HOW **NOT** TO SIGN A FILM CONTRACT

HOW **NOT** TO SIGN A FILM CONTRACT

KNOW WHAT YOU'RE SAYING YES TO

Roberta Marie Munroe

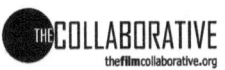

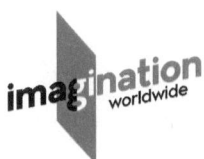

Here's to never having another lawsuit.

-RMM

Our Well-Thought-Out Disclaimer

Contents

Acknowledgments

Immense gratitude to Orly and Michelle for their contributions to this massive task, and to Kathy Susca for her support as our editor, helping to organize and ensure we created the book we set out to create.

Big thanks to Todd Hughes and P. David Ebersole for providing Butchie's Dream House as my gay writer's paradise, and Brian Vatcher and Cary Boisvert, for keeping me company with fancy cocktails and words of encouragement.

My biggest thanks is to the filmmakers, executives, friends, and colleagues who agreed to be interviewed for this book. Your commitment to helping other artists is invaluable.

Thank you!

Acknowledgment

Introduction

Who, What, Where, and Why

On a sunny afternoon in late April 2013, I emailed my dear friend Orly Ravid who, at the time, was in her final year of law school.

I was entering into a producer's contract agreement with a writer/director to produce their first project.

Previously, I had used a cobbled-together contract that outlined what I would do, what they would do, what the compensation would be, and what the start and end dates of our work together would be. I was emailing Orly to ask her to take a look at what I was about to send to the filmmaker and get her unofficial advice, which she generously gave.

What came to pass over the course of the next two years could be outlined in the Chapter 5: What's The Worst Thing That Could Happen? Enough said.

While the worst thing that could happen was happening, Orly and I were texting about it and she sent this text: "I have a great book idea for you. Follow up with a second book called How Not To Sign A Contract. LOL"

Once we stopped laughing, that text sparked a creative brainstorming session where we thought of all the people we knew who had been screwed based on the contract they signed, or worse, the contract they didn't have in place to sign. We also wanted to interview people who were saved by the contract they had in place.

We imagined all the honest filmmakers out there who had no idea how important a well-crafted and honorable contract was to their success and protection. Or if they did, they didn't know what one looked like. We wanted to show them.

We reached out to our community, and the lovely and talented Michelle Mower came on board with resources and a commitment to help her fellow filmmakers avoid the pain she herself had endured over the years.

We want this book to be your handbook. As noted in the paragraph that essentially translates into "you can't sue us" at the beginning of this book, this book does not constitute legal advice. It can't. No book can.

However, what this book can do is provide you with a font of information, professional advice, and a means for a much-needed education on many of the legal issues you will face when it comes to contract time in your negotiations.

And if you were not even thinking 'contract time' need ever come, think again.

Project development, production and distribution contain hundreds of moving parts, overseen by as many people, all of whom have various concepts of what The Truth is. We all speak different languages, colloquially and literally. What this book aims to accomplish is to present information in clear, layman's terms: the language of film industry contractual agreements.

That foundation can be summed up in one question: What does the contract say?

As my dear friend, and veteran producer, Effie T. Brown, has said to me many, many, many times, "Feelings are not facts."

Feelings are what engage you, and may be the reason you come on board to a project. The writer's feelings are what are outlined on the pages of the script. Scripts are mutable by their very construct.

With scripts feelings can, and do, make changes throughout the entire creative process. The beginning facts on the page may state, "White guy loses the love of his life and goes on a killing spree." Feelings could change that to, "Older black man unexpectedly becomes a widow, finds a new lease on life and opens a pre-school in Paris." Scripts are mutable.

Contracts are not mutable. Contracts don't have feelings. Contracts have facts, in writing, and more often than not, *in perpetuity*.

Orly explains that depending on what law governs it, if there is a dispute about meaning and there is ambiguity in the contract, evidence of intent may or not be admissible in court or arbitration. The words on the page need to be clear and mean what you understand them to mean, and others must understand the same meaning that you do (the other party and a judge or arbitrator if a dispute arises).

Good contracts are rigorously written, covering the widest scope of variables possible. They note the details of what all parties agree to in writing. That is their sole job. What are we both saying "yes" to, and what are we saying "no" to?

Whatever language you speak, this book will help you, your colleagues, and potential business partners create a common language of what the facts are that all parties are agreeing to.

In short, The Truth as it is meant to be understood and performed.

We're going to drill down into this ephemeral concept of what The Truth is throughout this book.

You and I may experience the exact same moment at the exact same time, but each of our Truths often end up being different.

It's the same with contracts.

We talked about the same contract, we read the same contract, we signed the same contract, yet should things go awry, our individual and contradictory understandings of what The Truth is can ruin relationships, make distribution of the film a nightmare, or in the worst-case scenario, land us in court.

I'm not a lawyer, but my best friend Orly Ravid is.

She, along with other veteran entertainment lawyers, will be guiding us in this book, explaining what honest and valuable legal advice can, and should, look like. Alongside them are filmmakers and industry veterans who share their experiences in order to make yours a good one. Or as good as it can be in this crazy business.

Knowing your rights, acting with respect for the process, and understanding the variations of film industry contracts is crucial to your ultimate success.

Why write this book now?

I wrote *How Not To Make A Short Film: Secrets From A Sundance Programmer* because after 5 years of watching film submissions, I could see clear and simple ways filmmakers were screwing themselves out of festival success.

As a programmer at Sundance, basic conflict of interest held that I could only help the people who were accepted into the festival, leaving behind the thousands who had no idea what they'd done right, what they'd done wrong, or how to fix it.

In *How Not To Make A Short Film*, I provided a step-by-step strategy for filmmakers – from script to screen to distribution – so at the very least, they would have a foundation of information for their next film. All they needed to add was talent.

And from what I gather from the thousands of filmmakers who have reached out to me after reading my book, it worked. I have firsthand experience that when you take the time to simplify and spell out for artists what avenue they should take towards success, they read it, they listen to your advice, and with talent, drive, and good fortune, they succeed.

And that is why I'm writing this second book.

And it is also why all the people who participate in it said, "Yes."

We want you to succeed from script to distribution, every step of the way.

And we want you to stay out of jail.

So let's find out: what are you saying YES to?

I

Before Somebody Dies,
Let's Start at the Beginning

Can't my producer deal with the contracts?

Uh, what about the contract you will need with your producer?

Keep reading.

WHAT IS A CONTRACT?

Everyone believes they know what a contract is because we sign them all the time. You sign a contract every time you update the software on your cell phone. Did you read it? Probably not. In fact, most of us spend an average of 6 seconds on the page where the agreement appears for our "Agree." (See: http://www.measuringu.com/blog/eula.php)

Do you know how many rights you sign away in those six seconds?

For many of us, the language in contracts is so unfamiliar that we psychotically avoid talking about it. Kind of like we avoid talking about math which can be, in the distribution world, perilous.

My friend, all a contract contains is language that provides all parties involved with an overview of dates, work expected, remuneration, consequences and conflict resolution clearly outlined should either party not hold up their end of the deal, and, importantly, where and under what law this conflict resolution will take place.

We all deserve a fair contract. One that imbues trust between parties, ensures both sides are adequately acknowledged and remunerated, and is a document with a beginning, middle, and end that all can rely on when things get hectic.

And in our industry, things *always* get hectic.

I will anonymously quote a dear friend who is a powerful producer with many years of experience. I mentioned this looming book deadline while we were on the phone deciding where to go and see Ryan Coogler's *Creed* and ended up talking about this book's content.

She was relieved I was writing something to help filmmakers with yet another layer of potential nonsense that befalls us all in this industry and shared her thoughts with us:

"I go home for the holidays and it's a disaster. My nephew, who is in several 12-step programs, was recently diagnosed with a variety of mental health issues. No one wants to tell my parents, but I can see he is on Lithium because I work in Hollywood where agents, managers, actors, directors, and all the crazy-pants people in between are on some kind of prescription cocktail (or should be). Having spent my entire life dealing with high-functioning geniuses for whom morals and integrity is a slippery realm, I am able to note when a deal is going sideways because the actor's agent has switched his meds and things won't smooth out for weeks. I know that if someone's assistant says the magic words, 'He's out for a few days this week,' that what's really happened is someone's Xanax prescription lapsed. And it's time to pull up that contract and call the legal department to discuss options."

If this veteran producer calls legal before moving forward, why do you think your producer should handle all the contracts?

Yes, your script is fantastic. Yes, you've got an exquisite eye for a visual medium. Yes, that money they're offering is the real deal.

But you're working in an industry where feelings can overwhelm facts, and astute filmmakers must know two things: How to make a great film, and how to make a great deal.

You must keep the facts in play, and let the feelings ebb and flow as is their wont.

How do you keep the facts in play? With:

    A. A contract.
    B. A contract that was written by a lawyer.

C. A contract that was written by an entertainment lawyer.
D. A contract that was written by an entertainment lawyer licensed IN THE STATE you want to adjudicate in.

The answer is D, and only ever D.

Sure your sister is a lawyer, and she's happy to help you. But if your sister is anything but an entertainment lawyer in the state where the contract is being created, her assistance can only go so far.

Just like Google, she can explain some basic boilerplate clauses, and perhaps some convoluted legalese in a contract because she went to law school and passed the bar. But she cannot help you understand, anticipate problems, or correct mistakes specific to a film entertainment contract deal.

The law is a vast and complicated arena. I have good friends and clients who are lawyers, who went to great schools and work at big firms. If I need a contract written or explained to me they can help me *because* they're entertainment attorneys versed in the contractual law I need help with. This is what they trained for, and these are the contractual agreements they work on all day long.

But if I needed them to help me sue my landlord over a rental disagreement they would be as useful to me as my mom: Providing compassionate listening with zero ability to give legal advice, but able to send me a few referrals. Maybe.

Think of it like this: The difference between an entertainment lawyer and a civil litigation lawyer (or an immigration lawyer, or a trademark lawyer, or a real estate lawyer) is like the difference between Alaska and Florida. Both are states in the union, but you will not find polar bears in Florida, or authentic *café con leche* in Alaska.

Make smart decisions from the beginning. What are you saying YES to?

You say, "But I'm just making a short film!" Or, "I'm just making an indie feature for less than $100k! I would have to spend almost 5% of my total budget on legal fees before we even go into pre-production!"

Consider it a tithe with a potential get-out-of-jail-free card attached. Because without the appropriate and correct contract, you will not get to pass GO and you will not collect your well-earned distribution dollars.

Julie La'Bassiere, CEO of BAFTA New York, offers advice on how to choose the right lawyer:

> "The best, or rather most important, thing that can happen when you hire an entertainment attorney is honest communication. As a potential client, you need to be upfront and transparent about what you are looking for the lawyer or firm to do for you, not be afraid to ask too many questions, and make sure you clearly understand what will or will not be charged for. Before you hire the lawyer or firm, YOU need to feel that you are getting honest answers – which are not necessarily the 'right' answers. Understand clearly what they can and cannot do for you, and that you can actually afford them. Start there and you are off to the right start."

Think of the "Legal" budget line as equal to your "Insurance" line. You would not go into production without insurance. Do not go into development without legal representation.

LONG FORM, SHORT FORM, MEMORANDUM OF UNDERSTANDING

Contracts take many forms: e.g. a Memorandum of Understanding (usually a short document that simply recites the deal points), a Short Form contract (as the name suggests, a short document, approximately 1 to 5 pages, reciting the deal terms), which is usually followed by a Long Form contract (approximately 10 to 40+ pages, which has all the standard terms and conditions, lots of legal definitions, and additional language).

I have responded to a speaking engagement request by email with the simple wording, "Let this email serve as my full understanding and agreement to our email correspondence thus far."

Obviously this isn't for directing or producing gigs. It's for simple, straightforward, smaller issue agreements; i.e. a professor sends me an invite to come and give a master class on festival strategy on a certain date, to commence at a certain time, for X number of dollars for X specific length of time.

My quick email back: Yes I agree to the fee and the topic, and I'll be at your location, at the time requested, for the length of time noted. Maybe I'll sign something in person (alongside a W9) but neither party needs a lawyer to oversee this exchange.

These types of contractual exchanges are not what we're talking about here. And I want to clarify that at the end of the day, some people will not sign your contract. They'll show up, they'll accomplish the work outlined in the contract they haven't signed, and because you're a filmmaker just trying to get the film in the can, you won't see this as an issue until you get to distribution.

At which point you will be exhausted, you will be ready to sell this baby, and when you find out all the contracts weren't signed, you will be sad. Or angry. Or both.

I spoke with former entertainment lawyer, Ed Reilly, who was legal counsel at Annapurna and worked for many years with Roger Corman. Something he said stood out to me, and I wanted to make sure we included it in this section: that long form contracts that are sent to actors rarely get signed before production begins.

I went back to Matthew Lessall, veteran casting director of Lessall Casting and current Co-President of the Casting Society of America, for clarification, and while it seems absurd, it indeed happens all the time:

> "That happened on a film that I both cast and produced. The lead actor didn't sign the long form agreement and I simply said, 'It's part of our deliverables that the long form agreements are signed.' I don't know what that's about. Sometimes I think it is the attorneys trying to give their actors an out if something happens, but at the end of the day, once the film is shot, they pretty much have to sign it. And you can just say, 'Look, you just worked on this movie for four weeks. We can't actually show this movie to anybody unless you sign it.' Once you make it personal like that, because you can make a phone call and call the actor and be say, 'What's going on? I just spent

four weeks of my life with you and you're not signing the agreement that was agreed to.'

I don't know what it's about, it happens all the time. The deal memo and the deal points that I negotiate with the agents are agreed to, and that is in writing, by email usually, so that's often good enough. On some level, that's proof that there was an agreement. They're reserving the right of their actors, usually, but the actor should sign it. It just doesn't make any sense. I don't know why they don't."

As Matthew and I spoke about this, I wondered, "If the other party doesn't sign the contract, does that mean I don't need to keep up my end of this unsigned agreement?"

Bueno, of course you do.

Orly Ravid, entertainment attorney and founder/co-executive director of The Film Collaborative, notes:

"What you have here is lots of ambiguity and a recipe for litigation if there is a dispute. By not having a contract signed, should there be arbitration or litigation, then the parties would look to perhaps not just the four corners of the contract but also all the drafts, communications/negotiations, emails, conduct, other statements, evidence of intent – all the stuff that would normally not be considered if a contract was signed and included the standard merger (aka integration clause) as discussed in our distribution chapter.

"But at the end of the day, the not-signing usually simply amounts to people acting as if that is the deal agreed to, but maybe one can argue otherwise if it comes to that. And if there is a disagreement, the resolve may come down to who needs whom more, and what they need from the other party to get what they want out of this film production.

"Though to be clear, not having an executed contract does not negate the existence of the contract – there is still the oral understanding, the performance/conduct under the terms of the contract that would be argued it should be enforced, and perhaps an argument of detrimental reliance in the reasonable expectation that the contract would be executed and that the parties proceeded as if it was all agreed to."

So it's clear that you may have an argument, should litigation occur, that this performer proceeded with all the work outlined in the unexecuted contract as though it was in force.

Do whatever you can to not be in this position, and ensure that your line producer has a complete bible of all executed contracts prior to the first day of production.

In this instance I can easily say you want to save yourself the aggravation and invest in peace-of-mind legal services before they become save-my-ass legal services.

Word.

YOUR FIRST CONTRACT

Is the one you have with yourself. Whether you are a director, actor, producer, costume designer, or editor - the contract you sign is the one you first agree to with yourself.

What are you capable of accomplishing for a production?

And more importantly, what are you *willing* to accomplish for a production, at what price point, and for how long?

In short, what does the contract say that you would be willing to sign with integrity?

The amount you would pay an entertainment lawyer to create or review contracts for your production is dependent on the length and scope of the documents involved. If you have a simple production, your legal requirements will also be simple, and thus the cost involved isn't going to break the bank.

This isn't a book on production. You do want to utilize an A to Z of production, and I strongly suggest reading Maureen Ryan's *Producer To Producer*, or watching the online video series *Lean Content* by Ondi Timoner (the only documentary filmmaker to be a two-time Grand Jury Prize winner at Sundance for her films *DIG!* and *We Live in Public*) and Eric Ries (the tech startup guru), available at atotaldisruption.com. If you're making a short film, you can always flip through my first book, *How Not To Make A Short Film: Secrets From A Sundance Programmer*.

Though, for the sake of clarity, I do believe we should walk through a bit of this initial process step by step, and later in the book we'll focus on the hoped-for end result of distribution.

FIRST STEPS

You hire a producer(s).

This is the second (only to yours) most critical contract.

What exactly do you want this person to do for you, and what does this person want you to do for them? Filmmaker Lydia Smith, Director and Producer on *Walking the Camino: Six Ways to Santiago*, did not get contracts in place with her producers before beginning development, and that came back to haunt her:

> "We shoot in 2009, in May. By May of 2010, she's not involved at all. That's 2010, so it's another three years before I finish the film. Once we started showing in theaters, she asked for her percentage, and I said, 'We have to reinvest the money.' She gave me $60,000 that came from her nonprofit. She has a board; they don't meet very often, but she felt like she was being incredibly irresponsible. She was scared that she was never going to get her 60 grand back. We worked it out. It was not pleasant. When we were finally doing this contract, if everybody had gotten what they wanted, I would have gotten 10%. I think it was never clear to them what their rights were. I'm sure from their point of view, they did donate a fair amount of time, but when you look at how much time was required - 2008-2013 - that's five years. So I worked more than full time for five years. None of them even worked a full year. In retrospect, I should have had a firm contract with them beforehand, but at the same time, what everybody promised they would do and what they ended up doing were totally different."

CRITICAL ITEMS IN A CONTRACT WITH YOUR PRODUCER

- Start and end dates
- Is this a Work For Hire, or shared ownership?
- Will there be assignments of preexisting owned copyrighted material?
- Is the fee noted in the contract a complete payment, or will this producer be allotted back end points?
- Is part of their fee deferred?
- And if yes, when do they get the balance (before the executive producers, financiers, or you)?
- Is it pari passu (sharing equally step by step)?
- Will the producer be the lead producer, or are you (or someone else) the lead?
- What exactly will their responsibilities be? Development? Fund raising? Script development? Casting? On-set producing? Post Production?
- What happens to awards? Is it different if it's cash or a trophy?
- If nominated for an Oscar®, or a similar award where there is strict criteria as to whom is designated, how is this resolved by the production?
- Festival travel, invitations, tickets, badges – who gets what?
- What are the repercussions should either of you fail to meet your contractual obligations?
- Do you have the right to termination, and under what circumstances?
- Should there be a dispute, do you want mediation, arbitration, or to proceed with litigation if necessary?

Choice of forum? (See Chapter 5 for more information on these points.)

Be very clear about what you expect this person to accomplish and outline it in the contract, in clear and precise detail.

OWNING THE RIGHTS

Something that filmmakers don't fully understand at the beginning: Who owns what?

You think you own your copyright because you wrote it. You registered it with WGA. It's your story.

Is it? Is that what the contract says that you signed with a producer or distributor?

Ed Reilly, former legal counsel for the production company Annapurna, insists that you make sure that no one has any rights that in any way affect distribution. Often, after buying a script where the seller represents and warrants that they have all the rights, it will come out that they don't – either you aren't the first company they brought it to, somebody has done a rewrite, they've gotten it from somebody else down the foodchain, etc. And in these cases, those attached people come out of the woodwork after you've purchased the script, or film, or project. So in order to get an approval on an insurance policy, you often have to settle with people if they have even an inkling of a claim, no matter how remote or tenuous. So it is crucial to ensure that people connected to the film have given up the results and proceeds of their participation throughout the creative process.

And he advises being very careful when you find yourself in the seller's position as well:

> "You just have to figure the first project, or couple, you're going to get screwed. Because you're going to be so thrilled that someone wants to come along and give you some financing for distribution rights or something that you'll give away the world. Because that's what they're going to ask for. And you have to decide, 'Do I want the movie made or not?' And you'll all feel cheated afterwards, and you probably have been. It kind of goes with the territory."

FAIR USE

Before beginning a discussion about Fair Use, Orly notes it is important to remember that Fair Use is not a right, it's a defense. It's a claim or argument one can make as to why one is not obligated to license the image or footage. Courts go through a four-factor test (analysis) to determine if the use is fair or infringing on a copyright.

P. David Ebersole is one of the principals at the The Ebersole Hughes Company. Over the last few decades, P. David and his partner in love and in business, Todd Hughes, have written, directed, produced, and executive-produced several well-received films. They include: *Stranger Inside* (HBO), *Room 237* (Indie), *Hit So Hard* (Indie), *Dear Mom, Love Cher* (Lifetime), *Reunion* (Indie), and most recently, *Mansfield 66/67* (Indie).

P. David describes the process The Ebersole Hughes Company went through regarding Fair Use for *Room 237*:

"Especially now, you pull so much stuff off the internet. And then, in the last moment once we realize what's in our movie, we need to do due diligence on every single image in the movie to figure out who is the copyright holder, even if it's positioned properly for Fair Use. We create a spreadsheet, *every image, every sound, everything we use in the movie has to be logged and reported* for the clearance and copyright lawyer and then the E&O insurance.

"This is the Fair Use conversation, which is more even than American law; it's international law. It's just called different things in different countries. If you are doing something for documentary/educational purposes, it does not matter that it's entertaining and fun, like some of our documentaries – you may use copyrighted material owned by other people as long as it is germane to your subject, and a few other clarifications upon that. You can't safely employ Fair Use without going through a very complicated legal process with a lawyer like Michael Donaldson, who wrote the book on copyright and clearance. There are only maybe five or ten lawyers who insurance companies will accept their letter saying, 'I have gone over this movie in detail, and I say the usages are Fair Use.' And then insurance companies, based on their letter, will give you insurance. Once you have that insurance, you can sell your movie.

"That's what we did for *Room 237*. Todd and I came in and created that possibility for clearance. First of all, we invested in finishing the movie, but we also understood the process well enough to be able to guide Tim [Kirk] and Rodney [Ascher] through the legal steps that it takes to get that kind of clearance. And their movie was complicated, because they never have a talking head on screen. Every single image is an image from something owned by someone else, so you create an excel spreadsheet, literally of every second in the movie, of what you see onscreen and what you hear. And then, Michael Donaldson's company in this circumstance, they go through your spreadsheet and they mark things: green – yes; yellow – needs more explanation; red – I don't think so. And you have to either clarify your arguments or re-edit the movie in an effort to turn your reds into yellows and your yellows into greens. When you think about a documentary and every image that appears onscreen, it's thousands of images that you have to create a spreadsheet, all the way through the whole entire movie, from first image to last image, and sound, and explain who it's from, who the copyright owner is, and why you believe it's Fair Use. Todd and I did the log for *Room 237* with answers from Tim and Rodney to help us, and in our other movies we do it. You are the only person who knows your own movie. Then you give it to the lawyers to go over it.

"So when we wanted to use a clip from the Academy Awards for *Dear Mom, Love Cher*, they made us couch the comment with so much information that nobody could say it was not Fair Use. They like to call it the sleeping judge. They say, 'If you put this in front of a judge who's falling asleep, and not paying attention, would he say this is Fair Use?' So you have to make it obvious, not, 'If you would listen to my argument, then you would understand.' Luckily that particular clip clearly needs to be there for the movie. Cher's mention of her mother at such an important moment in her life sets up everything that follows. But that was not enough on its own. We had to add commentary from Cher's interview with us to set up the clip. So when you want your legal team to accept something at Fair Use, think of the sleeping judge who's not paying attention. Our lawyers are making sure that if they are recommending that there is no loophole against Fair Use, that you have lived up to that. Because Fair Use only means that the lawyer and the insurance company agree that you are functioning within the realm of, the concept of, Fair Use, but it does not mean that the owner of the photo or video can't sue you and say, 'We didn't agree. That's my copyrighted material, and I don't like how you used it.'

"Having the right lawyer means a lot in that moment. Michael has been very good to us, and Dean Cheley, who has been our point person there, really have our back. They protect you, they look out for you, and they look to their own relationships to figure out how to smooth out what can be difficult.

"Think about *Room 237*, and that we used 20-something minutes of *The Shining*. We have major movie stars onscreen. The lawyer from Warner Brothers ran into Michael Donaldson at a party, and they were all just chatting and having a nice time and she said, 'Oh, and we need to talk about that *Room 237*.' And then they went out to lunch and they talked about it, and their biggest problem with the movie was not the movie, but the perception that the press was having that it was somehow philosophies of the Kubrick estate and/or Warner Brothers, because the press was reporting on it as though these were things that were real inside of the movie, as opposed to opinions from other people about the movie. And so they asked us for what we call the *exclaimer*, they call the *disclaimer*, that has to be onscreen thirty seconds before the movie starts, needs to be 20% of any poster, that says, 'Blah, blah, blah not the beliefs of Warner Brothers and/or the Kubrick estate, etc.' That's what they needed, and I think they expected a fight, and we said, 'Absolutely. We have no problem with doing that.'

"You're not looking for a fight. You're looking for everyone to be happy through contractual negotiations. You're not looking to make a grandstand play, you're looking to say, 'My side needs this, your side needs that.' And if you can keep your headspace in that instead of ego and you-can't-tell-me-what-to-do, then it all comes out a lot better. 'You can't tell me to put thirty seconds in front of my movie.' Well, yes you can, because you're the copyright holder to all of the stuff we're trying to use, so we're happy to comply."

MICHELLE MOWER TALKS TO AMY HOBBY OF TANGERINE ENTERTAINMENT

Tangerine Entertainment is a film production company focusing on commercially viable, critically acclaimed stories for all audiences, with an emphasis on female filmmakers and strong roles for women. Recent work includes Lucky Them, *starring Toni Collette,* The Last Laugh, *featuring Holocaust survivor Renee Firestone, and comedians Mel Brooks, Sarah Silverman, Carl Reiner, Gilbert Gottfried, and Judy Gold, among others,* Paint it Black, *directed by Amber Tamblyn, and the forthcoming feature,* Keep the Change. *Amy is also vice president of artist programs at Tribeca Film Institute and was a producer on the Academy Award™-nominated* What Happened, Miss Simone? *and TFC film* Gayby.

It's not uncommon for filmmakers to send distributors

incomplete contracts that lack the important language discussed in this book. Many of these elements would not naturally occur to a first time filmmaker, so it's extremely important to have an entertainment attorney review all agreements to ensure the production is protected from the beginning and the distributors have the necessary rights in place to exploit the property. This is particularly important when it comes to using intellectual property, such as music, archival footage, news clips, etc. Acquiring the rights to material protected by copyright is vital requirement for distributors. Without these rights, they will not be able to sell the film.

Let's look at a hypothetical example. You're making a documentary about a Jazz musician who died tragically at a young age. The musician never had children and most of his family are no longer alive. This talented artist and his music seem to be doomed to be forgotten. But you're going to change that! You're going to make a documentary about the musician's life and music. But there's a problem – you don't have the rights to his music, archival footage of his performances, interviews or even newspaper clippings. You know you need these things in order to tell the story properly, so you do your research and find out all the music rights are owned by various entities and individuals. In addition, the archival footage is owned by either a record label or television network. You don't have the money in your meager budget to license this essential content for your film. What do you do? Do you give up on the project? Do you let this musician's music fade into obscurity? Of course not! You must figure out how to acquire the rights to these materials.

Oftentimes, filmmakers assume they can't afford to license

content, so they don't try to acquire rights during production. They take the stance that they'll just make the movie and worry about securing rights when they land their distribution deal.

This is a bad idea for a number of reasons. First, you can't predict how much copyright material will cost because it's all negotiated on a case-by-case basis. Sometimes it's easier and cheaper to get rights to certain materials if you approach the rights owners as a poor, passion-driven filmmaker. If you wait until you get a distribution deal, the rights owner is likely going to demand a higher fee no matter how poor and passionate you are. Second, you may not get the rights. Then what? You have to spend money to re-edit the film, which will likely not make your investors nor your distributor happy. It could very well kill your deal. Third, creatively, you will have to figure out alternative ways of conveying the story – such as re-enactments – which will drive up your budget exponentially. You are setting yourself up for failure.

I know what you're thinking. What about fair use? I'm not going to delve too much into what constitutes fair use and what doesn't because that's not the focus of this book, but I will say fair use is one of the most misinterpreted and riskiest areas of producing, particularly on non-narrative projects. Fair use is a legal doctrine outlined in Section 107 of the Copyright Act (see end of this section for complete list of Fair Use factors) that stipulates particular circumstances in which intellectual property may be used without acquiring rights. It's a legal defense, not a production strategy. Academy Award nominated producer Amy Hobby, who has produced over 30 films, has used a mixture of licensed and fair use material in her productions. Hobby says she never goes into a production with the mindset that she will fair use material. "When I start a project," Hobby explains "I always assume that I am going to make best effort to license and clear material. I never like to hear from a filmmaker, 'Well, we'll just fair use everything.' That makes me uncomfortable, particularly if we don't know who the distributor is. Certain distributors may be more median on fair use and some will take some of those decisions to task, particularly for international distribution because fair use is interpreted differently worldwide. For instance, one of the ways you can fair use material is through parody in the U.S. The U.K. doesn't accept that as fair use guidelines. I like to err on the side of caution."

Erring on the side of caution is a smart approach to using copyright protected material. However, that doesn't mean you can't apply fair use when using copyright material in your films. For Hobby, it's all about weighing the risks with an attorney while working to ensure the story is told the way the director envisions. "I do support directors and I do support storytelling," Hobby continues, "and certain materials... there's just no way to clear it. I dig and dig and try and work. Sometimes there's ambiguity as to who owns the material and sometimes there's someone who, for crazy reasons, wants to block access to that material. If it is very important to the story, we should be able to use a certain amount of it to illustrate the story. I work very hard to support my filmmaker and help tell the story that we set out to tell. That's my job as the producer."

Even for experienced producers like Hobby, acquiring rights to certain types of material can be very difficult, particularly when dealing with major motion picture studios. "The biggest challenge for me on fair use was the film I did on Marilyn Monroe ("Love, Marilyn")," Hobby recounts. "We couldn't have gone into that with the assumption that we would fair use all her films from 20th Century Fox. The financier was interested in ignoring that because it would have been hundreds of hundreds of thousands of dollars. The issue becomes: you can't get those masters. And if you are going to do a film about Marilyn Monroe, 20th Century Fox basically feels they own her and created her and they have highest quality masters of those films. If you're going to make the ultimate film about Marilyn Monroe, you want it to look as amazing as possible. And 20th Century Fox will sue you." Stuck between conflicting interests – a financier who wanted to save money and a major motion picture studio with, presumably, an aggressive team of attorneys – Hobby had to take a hard look at her options and mitigate the risk. "After many conversations with the financier, we concluded that it was in our best interest to approach 20th Century Fox. I went to L.A. with the director and we sat in the offices at business affairs and met with the head of their archive in person. It took months and months and months to negotiate. It wasn't cheap in the end, but it was the right thing to do. And we got the most beautiful master footage ever, directly from their archives. It was best for the filmmaker and best for the film. And it was able to be monetized at that price point, so it worked out very well." But not all the copyright material in "Love, Marilyn" was licensed. Hobby continues, "There was some material in the film that we did fair use for various reasons. It wasn't like it was a policy straight up. It was weighing the pros and cons. A huge con is a 20th Century Fox legal team."

Fair use typically becomes an issue for filmmakers when they go to deliver the film because they can't get Errors and Omissions insurance, a requirement of most reputable distribution companies. Without proper licensing agreements and E&O insurance, you will not be able to get a distribution deal. Hobby suggests if you plan to use unlicensed material in a film, be very, very, clear about how the material constitutes fair use. Discuss the material with a copyright attorney who has experience with fair use cases. Send them a cut of the film prior to submitting to film festivals or distributors. In fact, Hobby recommends seeking your attorney's legal advice on sequences that involve unlicensed material throughout post production. She explains her approach, "In terms of process, on a project like Nina Simone or the Marilyn Monroe project, I like to begin talking to the fair use attorney sooner than later. As soon as we start working on the archival, I will email my fair use attorney and let him know I'm starting a new project. I get him on board, sign the paperwork. That way, if there's some footage that comes in and I start to feel worried, I can call him and have a conversation about it. Having those conversations early on is so helpful for process. I think the worst thing you can do is lock picture and send it to your fair use attorney. By then, everyone's in love with certain things, and then you have to go in and change things. The psychology of the producer/director relationship gets strained because the director wasn't informed that some things might have to be changed. That process is extremely important."

Attorney Orly Ravid agrees. "It's vital to consult with a fair use attorney who has a lot of experience in that specific area of law. It's a specialized field that has a lot of nuances that play out in a court room. So having an experienced attorney who has worked on fair use cases gives you an advantage. These attorneys know many of the players and can tell you which ones are litigious and which aren't." Highly experienced copyright attorneys can help filmmakers using unlicensed material acquire E&O insurance because they can explain legally how the material's use constitutes fair use. Having this knowledge and experience behind you throughout the production process allows you to make informed decisions that mitigates risk down the road and leads to a seamless delivery with your distributor.

*   *   *

The doctrine of fair use is codified in Section 107 of the Copyright Act and is meant to allow courts to avoid rigid application of the statute when it would stifle the creativity that the act was meant to encourage. Once again, fair use is a legal defense, not a right or a license.

The four factors to be considered in determining whether the use made of a work in any particular case is a fair use are:

(1) the purpose and character of the use, including whether such use is of a commercial nature or is for nonprofit educational purposes;

(2) the nature of the copyrighted work;

(3) the amount and substantiality of the portion used in relation to the copyrighted work as a whole; and

(4) the effect of the use upon the potential market for or value of the copyrighted work.

RELEASES

Filmmaker Lydia Smith had particularly complex obstacles to

surmount in getting the releases put together for her film *Walking the Camino: Six Ways to Santiago*, dealing with multiple languages, crews, and subjects while traveling through a foreign country. But having been a line producer for many years, she knew how critical it was to get them in place:

> "The tricky part was I had to do the releases in Spanish and English, and I think I even translated them into Italian and German. Because there were all these different people and they didn't want to sign. So I was really good about getting releases from people, I had people do that. And I knew enough to do that, as well as location releases. So got all those. And then there's this really beautiful church, and I would start that process knowing that we're going to be in Leon in a week. I would get somebody on it: we need to find out how to get permission, because it's a big church and it's really beautiful. And then the crew would just stroll in and start shooting and it was like, thank God I had gotten the permission."

OPTIONING

Stacey Davis, entertainment and intellectual property attorney at The Law Firm of Stacey A. Davis, goes over optioning and what you should be looking for as a producer:

> "The option process allows parties to share risk. A production company does not want to spend $25,000 on the purchase of the film rights to a book and then find out no one is interested in getting the movie made, whereas the option gives the producer the exclusive right

to buy the material (e.g. a book, an article, a screenplay, someone's life story rights) in the future once financing is secure.

"Always negotiate the acquisition agreement at the time you negotiate the option agreement. As the producer, you do not want to exercise the option and then be left with not the film rights to that *New York Times* bestseller, but the right to negotiate for the purchase of the material. I recommend structuring the option so that once the option is exercised the purchase provisions are invoked automatically.

"Another key consideration for producers is development of the optioned property during the option term. The option agreement should allow the producer to develop the optioned material during the term for such purposes as creating a proof of concept or commissioning a rewrite. The producer, however, would be wise to understand those rights do not extend to selling the developed property. For example, imagine an optioned script from a newbie writer needs a rewrite before it's ready to go to market, so the producer hires a more experienced writer to perform the rewrite. Unless the producer exercises the option to the script from the newbie writer (thus, purchasing the rights to the script), the producer will not be able to sell or exploit the revised script. Why? Because the revised script is considered a derivative work and the exploitation of derivative works is one of those 'bundle of rights' reserved to the author under U.S. Copyright law."

2

Mo' Money, Mo' Problems

All contracts deal with money in one way or another. However, the contracts that you create and/or sign are the ones that often seem the most terrifying. With the help of a few smart people, let me clarify a few of the possibilities you'll encounter.

CROWDFUNDING

We're not going to go into crowdfunding legal obligations because most independent productions are often financed privately. However, every crowdfunding site has very specific information as to what you're agreeing to when you sign up to raise money on their site.

Read it. Follow their instructions. Act with integrity.

Julie Keck, filmmaker and the Director of Media and Communications for the crowdfunding site Seed & Spark, lists the five most important things to know when beginning a fundraising campaign online.

JULIE KECK'S TOP 5 TIPS FOR COVERING YOUR YOU-KNOW-WHAT WHEN CROWDFUNDING

1. **Read the rules.** Don't let it keep you from doing what you want: Crowdfunding is a great way to get the cash to make your dream project. That being said, every crowdfunding site is different, so you need to know all of the nooks and crannies of their legalese. That's the only way you can know if you'll owe taxes on what you bring in or not. Don't just ask your friends; don't just read the FAQs. Read the rules.

2. **Back other people's campaigns.** When you're asking people to contribute to your campaign, you're asking them to put a lot of faith in you and the crowdfunding platform you're using. Be prepared to answer questions from your backers by backing the campaigns of others before you start your own campaign. That way you'll have a little experience under your belt when wary backers come to you with questions.

3. **Communicate, communicate, communicate.** If a campaign is successful, one of the worst things you can do is fall off the face of the earth. If you stop communicating with the people who contributed to your project, they might start to worry that you took the money and ran. Communicate with your backers as you move forward with the project by using the backer-messaging feature built into the crowdfunding platform you used. Also, share your updates and milestones via social media.

4. **Honor your commitments.** When people contribute to crowdfunding campaigns, they're not only signing up to see your film, they're also often choosing backer incentives. Make sure you deliver what you promised in your campaign, whether it's free downloads, t-shirts, DVDs, or other backer rewards. Incentives delivery can be taxing, but you can make it easy on yourself by offering primarily digital incentives.

5. **Make your damn movie.** Above all, if you said you're raising money to make a movie, you better make that movie. I haven't heard of anyone getting sued by a backer over an undelivered film... yet. But that doesn't mean it can't happen. If your production is delayed, communicate that with your backers. If it's not turning out the way you'd hoped, or if you blew your budget, or if your lead actor bailed, or if your editor turned out to be a dud, they need to know those things, too. I find that, overall, backers are very forgiving when they're looped in, so be honest about your progress and let your backer team support you in other ways. They supported your project because they're a fan of YOU, first and foremost, so give them a chance to give you moral support if things get rocky. They're on your side.

As laws around crowdfunding continue to shift, Orly shares:

> "You must obey SEC laws – this is not something you want to wing without an experienced attorney who is well versed on the applicable and current laws. I would hate to see your film be halted in distribution because of investor litigation. For example, now under the JOBS ACT one can be a crowdfunding investor, not just donor. You'll want legal advice on handling any investments and investor agreements."

PRIVATE INVESTORS

Private financing comes in several forms:

- Money from friends, colleagues and family that comes with "no strings attached."
- Money from private investors who are hoping to make their money back, plus a profit.
- Money from government or nonprofit arts organizations that comes with plenty of strings attached.

I've had some great experiences with private investors. These are often people who want to support independent filmmaking, want to support you personally, or simply want an Executive Producer credit on a project. Regardless of why they gave you money, you need to have an ironclad contract with them.

Here's why:

I produced a feature film by a first-time director who had a personal relationship with a wealthy businessperson who wanted to invest in this director's career. The investor was providing 100% of the financing in cash with no strings attached.

Before production, I met with them, and the financier told me, flat out, in person, "Roberta, you guys are the experts, you are the creative people. I'm not a filmmaker! And if I get half my money back, I'll be happy."

Me: *blank stare*

When I tried to put those words into writing in our contract, the director broke out into a cold sweat, and said, "I can't do that. We can't say that. They will take their money away."

I caved, and we moved forward into production with only this investor's word that they would accept and be happy with the film we made based on the script they invested in.

CUT TO: Two years later.

It was during this lengthy production and post-production period that I learned that the investor hadn't read the script. They were going on faith supporting this local filmmaker. It was a fairly non-linear, absolutely non-commercial story. We were never making *Fruitvale*.

It turns out they didn't like the final film and wanted us to do a pick-up shoot to add a scene to make it more "commercial," two years after original principal photography ended.

The rest of the team loved the final product and didn't want to change it, but we had to.

We didn't have final cut written into the contract.

So.

I'm on vacation in northern Ontario, driving up to my sister's cottage, and my cellphone rings. I pull into a strip mall parking lot and listen to this investor threaten our production's LLC, alongside the director and me personally, with a lawsuit if we didn't do as they requested or pay them their money back immediately. And this wasn't a hundred grand. The final number ended up being almost a million dollars.

We weren't allowed to submit our version to festivals and

other industry distribution platforms until we made the changes. So this film we'd all been telling the world about went into hiding for another 2 years while these changes were made.

Programmers and other industry folk were emailing and asking if they could see the film. Nope. Sorry, no you can't.

We made a decision to move forward without all the details in writing, and none of the production team had any idea it would all come down to this when we first started out.

Don't be us.

Have a contract that says what you all agreed to verbally, in meetings, on the phone, or over cocktails, and hire a lawyer to negotiate it.

When you're being offered the dream of a lifetime it's hard to push back. In fact, more often than not, it feels impossible.

But it won't be for your lawyer.

NETWORK TELEVISION

> "It's not that people are liars, it's that when it comes down to it, it's all fine to work from this altruistic, beautiful vision of what life is going to be like, but you need an understanding of what the rules are. And these rules are written down in a contract." –P. David Ebersole

On their film, *Dear Mom, Love Cher*, P. David Ebersole and Todd Hughes worked with a superstar and a TV network. P. David shares the experience of contract negotiations:

"*Dear Mom, Love Cher* we made with Lifetime. We financed it through a negative pickup deal, which is an old-fashioned concept. It was more of a '90s independent movie idea, and actually it's the same thing we did for *Stranger Inside* with HBO. The company provides the budget, which is essentially pre-paying to license it for their channel. They stay involved in all of the decisions and actually control the decisions, but from the point of view of the outside world, dealing with a US production entity, you – the filmmakers – are the decision makers.

"So The Ebersole Hughes Company had to carry all the liability for *Dear Mom, Love Cher*, and we carried all the liability for Lifetime, and thus we are the copyright owners on the film. They brought the idea to us, they brought the financing to us, we contractually delivered Cher to them, but in the end we had to do all of these extended negotiation contracts to make the project even happen. Between our agents, our legal, Cher's legal, Cher's personal people, Lifetime, their parent network, and lawyers involved from all sides, that contract was a complicated negotiation.

"Also, Cher is an executive producer on the movie, so our partnership with her was one of protection, compliance, and agreement. It's funny because there were contracts in every direction, and we 'hired' Cher, ultimately, for the movie. The Ebersole Hughes Company hired Cher, meaning that we had a performer agreement with her. That performer agreement had to be vetted by Lifetime and A&E, their parent company, in order for us to be able to sign. So that's what I'm saying about how complicated it all was. Anything that The Ebersole

Hughes Company was willing to agree to had to then be run by the network, even though it was a negative pickup deal. Even though ultimately, in the end, we own the copyright to the movie, what we were agreeing to had to be something that they also agreed to in order for us to get the money to make it."

The contract will not only help you know what you're saying "yes" to, but it will also provide you with a blue print as to what you are legally able to say "yes" to in ancillary agreements you have with other parties.

NONPROFIT & GOVERNMENT FUNDING

The level of bureaucracy within nonprofit and government funding is nothing short of extraordinary.

You can determine what the reporting responsibilities will look like for your project by the application process. The extent of the detail in the application process will mirror the level of detail you will need to provide in your final financial reports.

When you sign a contract with a nonprofit for funding you must consider them the same as you would a private or network (or studio) investor. You must use the funds as you stated in your application, as the organization's legal rules require, and you would be smart to consult with a previous funded project to fully understand what your legal requirements are... after you hire a lawyer, familiar with arts funding, to explain the contract to you before you sign and accept the funds.

For example, I know from experience that you cannot use government funding in most states for alcohol. This means that the budget line for your meals and entertainment cannot include alcohol. If you know me, you might be laughing, but it's also a "no" for your wrap party. You can cater the food, but the alcohol for your crew must go on your credit card.

Additionally, you often cannot pay people until all of their contracted work is completed. Depending on who your fiscal sponsor is (if you have one, if you don't, it's you), you will not get a check written to the post production house for the color timing until that project is complete. How often are you in the position of needing to pay a significant percentage up front to vendors prior to them commencing work? It's more often than you might remember, and the contract you signed essentially says you'll have to pay for that yourself and be reimbursed, or try negotiating with a vendor who doesn't know you from a hole in the wall and simply cannot afford to begin the work until they receive partial payment.

And with this kind of funding there is rarely room for negotiation. Their contract is their contract and the only reason (a great one to be sure) you need to hire a lawyer for this type of contract is so that you fully and completely understand, and are certain you are capable of fulfilling, all of its requirements.

The South Carolina Film Commission funds several projects throughout the year. Let's hear from Tom Clark, their Film Commissioner, with whom I have worked on several projects:

> "The first question to ask yourself is: Is the grant non-restrictive (can you do anything you want)? Must you hire scholars out of the budget or is there some minimum amount of research required by the funding authority?

Most don't allow you to buy equipment (never mind the alcohol!) so if you're thinking of buying the latest DSLR to shoot your project that cannot come out of the grant budget.

"My best advice: Do your due diligence, and read the grant rules or policies thoroughly, and then call the grant administrator. For our Film Commission and the granting agencies I've worked with over the years, as a grant applicant/recipient, I've found the grant officer or administrator is there to help you understand the process and prepare you for putting in the best application. Don't be intimidated by long, wordy applications. Take a deep breath and read them. Much of the language is boilerplate. Over the years, I've worked with NEA, NEH, local Humanities organizations, NSF, EPA, Energy, PBS, and many others. Every grant person at those agencies gave me much-needed intel to get my application as polished as it could be.

"If it is a grant with an agency that requires you to make stage checks or be involved with a grant office during your project, remember that they expect you to follow the rules. If you don't, the money could stop if it is a reimbursement grant. And you'll find yourself owing the agency back whatever monies they've given you thus far.

"Some federal grants seem as if they are awarded 'by the pound.' Keep the application reader in mind: if you load the paperwork with a bunch of superfluous information, it takes them more time to wade through your application and get to the bottom line. Grant readers don't appreciate that. Be thorough while, at the same time, succinct.

"It should also be noted that if you are unhelpful, ungrateful, difficult to work with, and it becomes clear you didn't read the application fully, when you come back to the table needing their money again, you can probably forget it. There are too many qualified, needy artists out there who can and do follow the rules, no matter how ridiculous they may seem, and that makes it easy to support them. Be that artist."

My friends, I'm with you when it comes to what's wrong with our industry and how filmmakers are often negotiated with. However, what we all need to remember is this: It's a business.

For the most part, those of you reading this book live in a capitalist world where people are seeking to make a profit. This is as true in the documentary world as it is in the narrative and animation world. And even in the nonprofit world, they have their bottom lines as well. They want to fund well-crafted projects that will help them fundraise for future grant programs.

I'll quote Effie T. Brown again and strongly suggest, "DBAD – Don't be a dick."

Once you move past self-financing, where the rules of engagement are your own, you have to get your big girl panties on and accept that the entities financing you are there to make a profit or elevate their own game. Yes, it might also be true that they want to support your creative efforts, but make no mistake: film financing has an absolute profitability expectation.

Remember the "win-win" contract negotiations strategy and you will be much happier for it.

3

Baby, You Better Have Their Money

The Casting Director. They read the script, they have great ideas for casting, you all have a meeting, you hire them, write them a check for X amount of dollars, and off they go to find the best talent possible for your film.

Except you don't have a contract clearly stating what this casting director is actually responsible for. You have 6 lead characters, 8 supporting, and 55 extras in your script that need to be cast.

Your casting director, based on the amount you paid her, believes she is only responsible for the 6 leads. The rest you must find on your own, or hire a casting director who focuses on supporting and background actors to deal with the smaller roles.

After you send her the secondary role breakdowns, and the number of extras you think you'll want, she sends you this update in an email:

> Hey Brilliant Filmmaker,
> Sorry, but I think we have a communication breakdown. I am only signed on to cast the lead roles. The rest you'll have to find by some other way or pay me another $XXXX and I can allot the time and additional staff needed to focus on casting the secondary roles of your movie.
> I wish I had the time to cast this whole film for what you've paid me, but I'm slammed and would need to hire at least one assistant to help out.
> I love the script, and you guys are amazing!
> Looking forward to working together.
> All my best,
> Ms. Casting Director

Now come the feelings.

What the hell? She's ripping you off! You had a meeting! You told her everything she needed to know about who you were looking for to be in your movie!

You had lengthy conversations about who these characters were, what you thought they looked like, acted like, needed to be.

You bought her lunch, and she hugged you when you said good bye!

Why would the CD think you only wanted her to cast the 6 leads and not the rest of the film? Because that's how this CD does business. She negotiates a fee based on the lead roles and assumes you are hiring another local CD and/or a background casting director, and have the resources to take care of the rest.

She's not ripping you off. You ripped yourself off by not having a contract outlining the facts.

You want to do your due diligence in all your contractual experiences, especially in this development stage of the project.

By the time you get to distribution (Chapter 5), you'll be your own best advocate at reading, writing, negotiating, and knowing when to sign or not to sign a contract.

Keep reading.

Matthew Lessall shares his process with us:

> "Alongside the actual work, being the lead casting director is also an artistic statement. It's saying that it's my job to maintain the artistic integrity of the work throughout the casting process. That means I can still be the main casting director while only technically casting the five lead roles. I am often casting the whole film or television show, however the roles of 6-20 are being handled by another casting director, with me signing off on whom they propose we cast. I take that list and discuss it with the director and/or producers.
>
> "Listen, the local casting director has to take over at some point unless you have a larger budget to pay a high enough fee to my company that I can utilize additional staff to accommodate your entire film's needs."

TERM – LENGTH OF ENGAGEMENT

One of the top items to look for in the contract is the "Term." How long will this person work on your project? 3 months? 6 months? 1 year? Until it's cast (directed, produced, shot)?

They're going to work on your project for as long as the Term says in your contract. When I'm producing "for hire," I make sure it's clear in our contract exactly how long I will work on this project before we have to renegotiate the agreement. The reasons may be obvious, but to be clear, Matthew Lessall spells it out for us:

> "You can't be on a film forever, so the term forces things to happen by setting an end date. I like to have the end date in the 'Term' paragraph of the contract to be at the end of the first week of pre-production, or the end of the first week of shooting, so that there's at least a week overlap. It forces the filmmaker to understand, 'We're making a movie by this date, and we have to make decisions.' Because if you're going to wait for George Clooney's people to decide if he wants to be in your film, you're going to have to push, but the agreement between you and the casting director stays the same. That means you're going to go into overages, and the contract has to be negotiated again because the Term of the agreement is ending on such and such a date.

> "You can't take for granted that you can just move on, and the rest of the crew you've hired will do the same. It happens all the time, but it doesn't mean that I should keep working on it for free. Because, in truth, I am working on it, whether you've pushed the dates or not.

Because usually a casting director is hired before payroll services, before pre-production, and so in the past it was very loosey-goosey and now I don't do that because I want concrete decisions to be made in the time frame that we agreed to. The time frame that I've carved out for your project in the midst of all the other projects I'm casting."

We used Lessall Casting to cast a feature I produced called *Warrior Road* (written/directed by Brad Jayne, executive produced by Denis Gallagher and Charliewood Pictures). In the initial phases of contract negotiation with them, Matthew Lessall suggested we find a local (to South Carolina) casting director who would be responsible for the secondary characters, as well as overseeing the background/extras casting director in each location we were shooting in.

It worked like magic. Our local casting director, Matt Sefick, found us fantastic additional cast, who were willing and able to work as locals. And being from the area, he was also quick to link us up with a local extras casting director who handled our background actors with speed and professionalism.

CASTING DIRECTOR TOP CONTRACTUAL CONSIDERATIONS

- How many roles are they responsible for?
- How much are you paying them, and for how long?
- Are you responsible for additional miscellaneous costs (postage, couriers, phone, travel)?
- Are they being offered profit participation (back end points) as part of their fee?

- Will you invite them to premiere screenings and provide festivals tickets and/or travel?

- If this is a union, how many weeks and fringes are being offered?

- Are they authorized to speak on behalf of the production to agencies and management companies?

- Do you have a "catch-all" clause stating that the CD shall provide standard, customary casting director services?

- How are they to be credited (i.e. single card in main titles, same font and duration as others)?

- Under what law is the contract governed (i.e. the State of California) should you find yourself in court?

- Have you included an arbitration clause?

Allow the casting director to do what they're good at. Allow the costume designer to do what they're good at.

Give them the freedom to be the artists that you want them to be.

Of course everything has to get approved by the producer, and of course everyone signs off with the director, and everybody has to be on the same mission and be on point, but within that, the more you have (in writing) detailing their duties, the less you need to be worried about what the end result of this exchange will be.

EVERYONE ELSE – YOUR CREW

The above list of items in a casting director contract are also the same for all of your crew. You would obviously change the first line for each agreement, but the rest are invaluable clarifying clauses you want in everyone's contract.

For example, if you don't have a Deal Memo/Contract Agreement with your director of photography, they will own the footage they shoot. The same goes for your sound recordist. You will not have to ask too many filmmakers before you find someone who has been in a legal battle with their DP or Sound Person.

Effie T. Brown is a prolific film and television producer whose resume includes *Rocket Science, In the Cut, Things You Can Tell Just by Looking at Her, Everyday People, Desert Blue, Real Women Have Curves, But I'm a Cheerleader, Project Greenlight*, and she will be an Executive Producer on a new TV show called *Star*. Effie describes the importance of outlining your intellectual property and including non-disclosure agreements with your crew:

> "I think now it's different with crews with the advent of social media, because you have people saying, 'Well, I'm the DP, what if I take a still and I post it on Instagram or Facebook? Do you own that, or do I own that?' Just because I show up to work doesn't mean that you own every single thing about me, unless it's in my contract. We're now dealing in worlds where everything is wrapped up. Who you are, what you do, where you work, and what you're doing at that particular place of work all is a part of something bigger now, because you have Facebook, Twitter, SnapChat, etc. Nowadays you have ancillaries like behind-the-scenes, concept reels, and stills. Maybe you did a job and you were a DP or a production designer, and now you're mounting this other movie, and you want to use the work that you did as a concept reel for this

other project. Technically, you don't own that other stuff if you signed away your life on the first project. All of that stuff becomes intellectual property. You have that moment where you're like, 'Well shit, everything is really interconnected and there are a lot of gray areas.' How are you going to enforce it? But what's interesting, when you start seeing these big movies like *Star Trek*, there's a non-disclosure agreement and they tie a dollar amount to it: 'If we can trace back to you that you did it, your agreement pay is $10,000.' And people sign it."

Once again, we remind ourselves that Feelings are not Facts. And anytime you have human beings involved, you'll have feelings involved.

Imagine this: you find the DP who shoots in a style that is going to work perfectly for your film. You two work together for months on tone, shot lists, floor plans, and dates of production.

They become one of your creative soul mates on this project… until they don't.

By the time the shoot ends, they hate the producer, or worse, they hate you, and they've fallen off the face of the earth with a memory card full of dailies from the last two days of shooting.

It gets to a place where you need to hire an attorney, whose first question will be, "What does your contract with them say?" But you, in the heady days of creative soul mate love, didn't make the DP sign one. You paid them a flat rate (or they worked for free), and nothing bad had ever happened prior to the production so you assumed they'd be on board through thick and thin.

I don't need to imagine this with you because it happened to me it real life. On day 2 of a particularly stressful shoot, the DP threw multiple chairs at me, all the while calling me a "See You Next Tuesday." They owned the camera and a lot of the equipment we were using.

It was only by the grace of God that my UPM co-owned the camera and equipment with this person. So they and the rest of the camera crew were able to physically remove the DP from set and keep all our drives and equipment from leaving with them. I made the Steadicam operator the DP and we forged on to make a great film that went on to do well in the world.

But in a much more terrible scenario, without a work-for-hire contract and our camera equipment rental agreements, that DP could have taken everything with them and a court battle would have ensued.

I'm not telling you to only be smart and remember The Truth, but to also be a good businessperson. The foundation of a great film is all of the business aspects that go along with filmmaking. And contractual agreements are an imperative component to this structure.

4

Viola Davis Probably Won't Sign Your Contract

Contractual negotiations with actors are rarely negotiated by you or your producer. They're negotiated by the talent's agents/managers and the casting director. And this is true for a very good reason: they're able to do it without emotion. You're not. They're dealing with facts.

You think you are. But you're not. Neither is the actor.

You're in your feelings of excitement to have this talent in your film. They're dealing with the same feelings from a different standpoint.

They'll promise you all kinds of things they simply cannot deliver. Sure, they can do a week of rehearsal under SAG-

AFTRA's radar, and a week before that date, you hear from their agent that since it wasn't listed in the contract, and thus no one knew about it, their client is booked on another job across the country. It happens all the time. ALL. THE. TIME. Unless you have a contract detailing all the dates the actor is promised to your production.

It's the job of the casting director to ensure that they're the right actor for the role, they're available for the dates of your shoot, they're willing to work for an agreed-upon rate, and they are able to perform all aspects of the script.

It's the job of their agent to ensure their clients get paid a fair rate, work under circumstances that are safe and comfortable, and that it is a SAG-AFTRA signatory production.

Matthew Lessall agrees:

> "The director should only talk about the creative part of the film. They should never, ever get into any contractual conversation. That's my advice to the director. Just talk about the film, and then relay what you talked about with the actor to your producer who will then have a heart attack because they're like, 'You said what? We can't deliver that.' And then that's the job of the producer and the casting director to back pedal what may have been your hope and dream, but is actually an expectation that can't be met by the production."

Listen, your job as the director is to make sure the actor can perform the role as you intended it, or better. Your job as the producer is to ensure the budget, crew, cast, and all of the contractual agreements will be conducive to a great production and distribution. We all know that there is a job title for a reason, and your casting director, your producer, and the talent's representation are no different. Let them do their jobs – your film's survival depends on it.

Michelle Mower, President of international sales and distribution company Imagination Worldwide, shares:

"In the early 2000s, I worked as the Program Coordinator for a non-profit media arts organization called Southwest Alternate Media Project (SWAMP). Their mission is to promote the creation and appreciation of film and new media as art forms of a diverse, multi-cultural community. Part of my job at SWAMP was to develop professional development programs targeted to independent filmmakers and film professionals. In 2004, I started SWAMP's annual Business of Film Conference, that takes place every fall at Rice University in Houston, Texas. Why would an arts organization host a business conference?

"The idea came after a call I received from a frantic producer. She was very upset because her lead actor quit a week into production. She was worried about all the footage that would have to be reshot. I asked her if she had gotten a deal memo with the MIA talent so that she would have something in writing as recourse. She didn't. The craziest part of this story is that this so-called 'producer' also happened to be an attorney. Granted, she wasn't an entertainment attorney, but she still should have known better than to go into a feature film production without all essential contracts signed. I realized the problem wasn't that she didn't understand the importance of contracts. It's that she approached the production as a hobbyist – not a professional. Had she approached the production as a business instead of a hobby, she would have made sure she had all her contracts signed before shooting a single frame.

"For distributors, one of the most important things we want in a talent deal memo is a Waiver of Injunctive Relief (also known as a no-injunction clause, read more about this in Chapter 5) that prevents talent from holding up the film's release for any reason. I know it's hard to believe, but actors can be very self-conscious. They tend to have a lot of concerns about their image, especially on camera. If a film is bad or, worse, if their performance is bad, it would not be beneath them to attempt to stop the film's release. There is actually a precedent for this. *Don's Plum* is an example of how famous actors (Leonardo DiCaprio and Tobey Maguire) can leverage their star power to block the release of a production they were involved in –the film is still not available in the US and Canada to this day. It happens. Don't let it. GET IT IN WRITING."

Believe me, Michelle is right. I've worked on projects where, prior to hiring a casting director, the director knew the actor and promised them a bunch of stuff that simply wasn't possible given the budget we were working with.

I could easily retell several stories of actor deals gone wrong because the director thought they knew what they were doing.

Once I had an actual casting assistant who was directing the project I was producing, and with all the knowledge they had, the deal they made with the principal actors screwed us budget-wise.

For example: You have an A-list actor who says yes to your indie project, for the SAG-AFTRA low budget agreement daily rate and you're thrilled. And you should be. What you should also be is aware that just because the talent said yes to the lower daily/weekly rate, it doesn't mean their team will.

I had an exceptional experience with the talented and wonderful Lily Tomlin on a short film production. She loved the script, and she came on board for pennies. The director dealt with his casting director friend and we signed the deal, dancing in the streets that we had this legendary actor. The fine print: like any professional artist of her level, she only works with her own hair and makeup team.

And their daily rate combined was a third of the total budget we had for the entire project.

Of course Lily is going to say yes to a talented production team she wants to help get their film done on a tiny budget, but her seasoned team probably will not. This is not something we considered until we were in touch with the fine women who take perfect care of Lily. We assumed since Ms. Tomlin was working for the SAGindie rate, so would her team. Nope.

Yes, we raised the money to ensure Lily was treated like the queen she is, but it would have been a lot easier had we known about this extra money required long before we did. Had we gone forward with a proper contractual negotiation, we would have been aware of this bump in the budget. It would have been in Ms. Tomlin's contract that we use her hair and makeup team, and only them.

It's the same for accommodations, flights, assistants, car services, etc. You want your talent to feel well rested, well cared for, and respected for the work they're going to bring to your film. All of their needs must be discussed up front, and be in writing in the contract.

However, it often happens that even when all their requests are considered and an agreement is reached, the talent refuses to sign. Michelle describes her frustration of feeling like the entire project is at risk:

> "On a film I produced and directed, one of my actresses was advised by her attorney not to sign her deal memo until the production was wrapped. I was unaware at the time that this was a common practice in the industry. The actress kept saying, 'Talk to my attorney,' when we asked her to sign the agreement. I won't lie, I took her refusal to sign the agreement personally. Hadn't we gelled in our meetings prior to production? Didn't she say she was excited to work with me? She even said she was fine with not getting her own trailer, but NOW her attorney is demanding one. WTF? I thought the actress was being difficult, but the truth is she was just a kid who was doing what the attorney told her to do. If I had an attorney, I could have let them battle it out so I could focus on working with my actress on, you know, her performance. And that's what I should have done. But I didn't know what I didn't know. So I flipped out instead. I told my work-for-hire producers to get the agreement signed or I would shut down the production. And I meant it. I wasn't going to risk spending another cent without her signature. She eventually signed, but the experience put a strain on our working relationship. As a director, I should have never let that happen. As it turned out, the fears and sleepless nights were for nothing. The film got a

distribution deal and has been seen all over the world. My actress and I now have a friendly relationship. I credit her all the time for my success. I would work with her again in a heartbeat."

A basic contract that I have seen, and have used in shorts with the actors, is just a simple deal memo. Likeness, in perpetuity, in all territories, $100 a day for these days, stills, and for short films I don't include anything about premieres or festivals (except to say that that actor's presence would be appreciated but not paid for).

Once you are in the feature narrative world, the contracts often become more complicated, more expensive, and thus more in need of legal oversight. The variables of what an actor's representation may request for their client is endless. What you want to know is what the basic list looks like, what your budget can bear in terms of special requests, and when to flat out say "no" and start looking for another actor who has lower expectations from a low-budget production.

A COMPREHENSIVE CONTRACT FOR TALENT SHOULD INCLUDE:

- Term: Begin and end dates of engagement
- Rehearsal dates, locations, and times the actor is expected to participate
- Production dates: Wherever possible, this should be inclusive of the entire production, giving you flexibility on the dates you need to shoot their scenes in case of budget constraints or simple acts of God

- The salary details
- The name of the role they will be performing
- Your commitment to having Liability and Workers' Compensation Insurance for the duration of the production, including rehearsal dates
- Their full name (as they wish to be credited if different from legal name)
- Mailing Address
- Phone Number (personal cell, not their agent's)
- Email (personal, not their agent's)
- Social Security number (regardless of how much or if they're being paid)
- Name and Likeness: They sign away rights to the production so that you can do whatever you want with the footage they're featured in, in all formats, in all territories, in perpetuity.
- Is a specific wardrobe required, and if so, will it be furnished by the production?
- Note whether or not you will pay for cleaning if the actor brings their own clothes.
- How the actor is expected to arrive at set (are they driving themselves, or are you sending a PA to drive them to and from set)?
- Are they to arrive to set with hair/makeup ready, or are they being taken care of by the production?
- Will they be given private space during production (trailer, separate room)?
- How they will be credited (single card, shared card, credit roll)?
- Will they be on the marketing materials (poster, flyers for festivals, website)?

- Will the credit on the film differ from that on the poster and other marketing materials?

- Health and Safety: You agree you will make best efforts to ensure they are taken care of during the shoot.

- You commit that you will provide adequate food and drink during the shoot.

- Waiver of Injunctive Relief: See Orly's Red Flag Cheat Sheet in Chapter 5 for more on this clause.

- Are they expected to do press? What kind (radio, print, on camera)? If on camera, who is responsible for their hair, makeup, and wardrobe?

- Are they expected to attend the premiere? A specific festival screening? Who is paying for the travel and accommodations? Is there a per diem involved?

- If there is a cash award for "Best Performance," how is this money disbursed?

- Consider including an NDA, just like in your crew agreements.

If you are in an arena that your film may get into top-tier festivals, some of the points above are particularly important to consider for your film's promotion:

- Interviews and appearances for TV, radio, print, events, etcetera: How many events should they do, and when? If they require hair, makeup, and wardrobe, get clear on who pays for that.

- Festival attendance and theatrical openings: Try to get them to commit to attending these important publicity events, subject to non-availability. If they are hesitant, you might ask them to make "commercially reasonable best efforts" instead of a flat-out commitment. Remember, you'll need to include, in writing, who is footing the bill.

• Social media promotion: This can be especially advantageous if you have high-profile talent with a loyal following online. If you have an NDA, it would also come into play here.

If you can think of it, it should be in the contract.

SAG-AFTRA (UNION) AGREEMENTS

Now, there are a ton of sample agreements online, but I would say the most important elements beyond the list I wrote above are what SAG-AFTRA insists upon.

A person could write an entire book solely on the process of filling out their paperwork so suffice it to say: Go to their website. Download the package and READ IT CAREFULLY. You don't need a lawyer to go over it for you because SAG-AFTRA assigns a staff person to walk you through the process once you apply. Though you will need a lawyer once you begin the negotiations with your talent beyond what you're legally required to do as a signatory project with SAG-AFTRA. I promise you, after you do it once, it will be a piece of cake for all your future productions.

To back this belief up, I reached out to Darrien Gipson, Executive Director of SAGindie:

"Keep in mind that the beginning of using contracts to hire the professional talent for a low-budget film actually started in the late '60s. But the real push of it was that in the '70s, kind of the heyday of the independent film movement, nobody was hiring professional talent, or people were having to do it quietly and under the table, because they couldn't afford to pay, even with the contract that was designed to help them, or they were too afraid of having to deal with this big, monolithic, bureaucratic entity. They were like, 'Oh, they're going to make us do this, that, and the other, they're going to shut us down.' As the owner and ED of the SAGindie Program, which exists to give factual information to filmmakers on what they can and cannot do, I work to show how easy it can be to become a signatory production. Ain't nobody trying to shut you down. We want to help you succeed. It seems complicated at first, but really it's not, and for professional actors who are in SAG-AFTRA, they still can't do that film if the film's not signatory. In the last 15 or so years, people have taken a hard look at actors who go against their own union, because why are you in it if you're not going to listen to it? You can't ask somebody to protect you here, but then ignore them when you feel like it. Push the production to become signatory so you are protected, and the production is elevated."

I said it in my first book, and I will reiterate my belief here: You always want to utilize SAG-AFTRA on behalf of the production, and absolutely on behalf of your actors. Sure, some union actors may work with you under the table, but as I have mentioned from the beginning, your pristine contractual hygiene is the foundation towards successful distribution.

If you are lucky enough to get your film a distribution offer, but you don't have locked-in agreements with your talent and have to go back to them (or worse, go on bended knee to SAG-AFTRA) you will be sorry, and it might screw you out of a great distribution deal or make it a lot more costly than if you had simply paid the initial costs to be a signatory project.

Darrien continues with clarification on what it means once you sign an agreement with SAG-AFTRA and why it's important WHO signs that agreement:

> "SAG-AFTRA is going to ask you for some very basic information. Who is your bottom-line person? And that person better be someone who you know will see it through. So many times when things happen and things go wrong, it's because the producer that they had sign all the paperwork then disappears, and now they can't get the last of their paperwork in. So that's not your lowest-common-denominator producer who you don't care about. This is somebody who has to be essential to this project, and so it's important to have a person who you know will be there from beginning to end, and through it all be the point person. We spend a lot of time explaining that this is what it's going to cost you, how to send in the paperwork, and so if we give all that information to the producer who is no longer with the production by distribution, it will be all on you. Something to note is if it's a short, you actually don't have to pay anything up front. It is deferred, and it's only due if you get distribution."

I'm going to jump in here and strongly suggest you pay everyone their daily/weekly rate during production and do not defer an actor's (or anyone else's) pay. In this indie film business, most people are not in a position to not get paid while they're working for you. Plus, not only is it cleaner for the production to be paid in full with the talent when it comes distribution time, it's often crucial that you have all your t's crossed and i's dotted with SAG-AFTRA in order to even begin to negotiate a distribution deal.

Yes, it's an increase in the budget, because whether the production costs you nothing or it costs you $250,000, you are required to pay actors $125 a day for every day they work, plus pension and health.

The thing that usually trips up filmmakers is that whatever your budget is for your talent, you're going to need to have 200% of that talent budget. If you have just $1,000 budgeted for your cast, you're going to need to give SAG-AFTRA $1,000 to hold in a security bond, and you're going to have to have another $1,000 to actually pay people out during production. Once all the talent has been paid, SAG-AFTRA releases the bond funds back to your production, however that can (and usually does) take several weeks.

MFN –MOST FAVORED NATION CLAUSE

Put simply, MFN means that you are offering all the talent (and oftentimes other ATL and crew) on the project equal contractual treatment, including pay, accommodations, flights, and any other contractual provision that is being offered to anyone performing in your film.

Most talent (or their representation) requests this clause, though few get it.

The main reason is budget.

If you have an MFN clause in your talent's contracts, and an A-list actor comes on board and they require first class airfare, accommodations, childcare, and separate accommodations for their personal staff, you would be legally required to offer that to every other actor.

Are there ways to get around this? Sure. Are they legal? No.

So let me share what Matthew Lessall had to say around this issue that is legal, and will save you aggravation in the long run:

> "I always try and find language that isn't MFN. Or if there's MFN, it's only on certain deal points. Be very specific in the contract that this is not an MFN contract but there are going to be deal points where you use the term MFN solely for those deal points.

> "The beauty of this business is you can make all that up on a case-by-case basis. There is no one way of doing things. Yes, there is a standard, but you could say, 'Look, I'm going to give you first class flights from LA to Charlotte (5-hour flight) but economy from Charlotte to Charleston (less than a 1-hour flight).' The intent is that of course you want to provide everyone with the highest level of accommodations, or flights, or whatever. You tell the talent, 'Of course, whatever we can do to make this experience great for you, we're going to do.' But that isn't MFN. That's 'best efforts,' and those best efforts will be different for every actor's needs. You will do whatever the budget allows to ensure they're comfortable. So let's say instead of offering talent first class or business class, you offer everyone some sort of premium economy. That

way, with a full-price ticket, an upgrade can easily happen closer to the departure date. It gives an actor options, and it also makes you look like you are, in fact, making best efforts. It's here in the beginning of the negotiations where your casting director comes in and says, 'I can't put the MFN in the contract because there's a chance I'm going to fly in a British actor who's going to be great for the film,' and if so-and-so actor doesn't want to do it because Mr. British actor might get a better class of flight than them, it's good to know that's what type of actor they are. That's what you're dealing with. You want to take note when an actor is insisting on special treatment that is outside your budget. If you're struggling with them during the contract negotiation, you will find they haven't changed much once you get on set."

I would also say this really is the arena where your casting director and entertainment attorney are going to save you a ton of headaches. It's their job to negotiate these items on behalf of the production. Sometimes an actor will really just want to make sure they're staying at the same hotel as the other key talent, but don't really care where they're sitting on a 3-hour flight. Your casting director and attorney can parse out the MFN details so that this one deal point, the hotel, is MFN, however the other deal points (flights, drivers, back end points, etc.) are not.

The casting director knows what's possible, they know the agents and talent better than you do, and this is what they do all day, every day.

Let them do it.

NUDITY CLAUSE

Here is one arena that a contract isn't going to save you once you're on set. There is no universe where you can force someone to take their clothes off or perform a sex scene, even if they signed a contract that says they would.

Effie T. Brown agrees:

> "You can't force somebody to do something that they don't want to do. That's why, being a producer, your job is to 1) bring people to the table that are amenable to doing what you need them to do, and 2) be able to cajole, convince, and love up someone enough to do it. Actually, what's even more important is for them to see the logic of why you're asking them to do it. If you're a good producer, director, whomever, you'll also be open to be like, 'Oh, you know what? That person's right. None of this makes any sense. There's no reason for it. You're right, that is totally exploitative.' It's a conversation, a collaboration, and I think a lot of times, in my experience, shit goes sideways because there's a loss of trust. When you make those deals, you don't have your camera team, you don't have your sound person yet, and all of those people are in the room. That's why you have closed sets, and you try to make it as comfortable as possible."

This isn't the army. It's a creative endeavor where the ability of a director and producer(s) to inspire the talent to come along for the ride is paramount.

Few actors agree to do nudity in your film and then get on set and say, "No."

Of all the times I've had actors in nude or sex scenes, or heard from other directors and producers that the scene went south, it was always because the actor didn't trust the production to treat them with respect. The director was too inexperienced, didn't know what they really wanted, or was asking too much from the actor; the producer was a creep and wouldn't give the actors privacy; the DP wasn't listening when the actor asked to not be filmed from a certain angle; or the other talent in the scene wasn't being professional.

I asked Matthew Lessall about it during our interview, and here is his Nudity/Sex Scene List to follow for best end results.

NUDITY AND SEX SCENE PREPARATION

- Have a detailed shot list that you go over with the actor several times before you're shooting the scene in question.
- Have a well-crafted storyboard and show the actor exactly what the camera is going to see, for how long, and how close up you will be shooting.
- Respect an actor's need for privacy; clear the set of all non-essential crew.
- Listen when an actor gives you notes on how they would like to be seen.
- Ensure the costume design team is familiar with merkins and other cover-ups.
- Ensure the actor wears the cover-ups – in fact, I would insist on it.
- Give your actors the "CUT call" (see below).
- Act with integrity, and keep your word.

On one of my many soul-crushing round trip drives between Palm Springs and Los Angeles I was listening to Alec Baldwin's podcast "Here's the Thing." He was interviewing Cary Fukunaga about the first season of True Detective. Cary shared that for him, the actor always has the right to "call the scene." So if there's a sex scene, or a rape scene, then it's the actor who holds the right to say, "Cut." They have the "cut call." And I am certain it makes the actor trust Cary and the production in a way that helps them get through the scene that works for all involved.

Yes, they signed a contract saying they would do nudity and/or a sex scene in your film. Nonetheless, it is essentially unenforceable, because no one has time to try to sue an actor while in the midst of production.

Don't be an asshole. Be a Cary Fukunaga.

DEFERRALS, BACK END POINTS, "IF THIS, THEN THAT" CLAUSES

How often does it happen that an actor will say, "Yeah, I'll work for $125 a day, however, I want points on the back-end"? Or, "I will work for $1,000 a day, of which you can pay me $125, but I want it deferred upon increased financing or a sale"?

Orly explains: "When talent is either not being paid what they want up front or simply has the star power to demand back end, then they will get back end percentage (aka 'points') of gross receipts or the net profits (the definition of which is critical). These days points seem par for the course, especially for A-list talent, but it may also be a way to get talent that you cannot afford on the front end, and this could incentivize promotion of the film during release."

Everyone I spoke with, many actors included, agreed that adding complicated "if this, then that" clauses in contracts wasn't necessary and more often than not, wasn't valuable to the negotiating process. This is because most independent films do not go on to distribution or make their money back, and thus there is nothing to profit-share. However, if you are in negotiation and the talent's representation wants back end points or "if this, then that" clauses added, do it. But be smart about what you're offering, and really be clear about who will be responsible to follow up with SAG-AFTRA.

5

What's the Worst Thing
That Could Happen?

Unfortunately, when it comes to distribution, many filmmakers are so exhausted, beaten down, and broke that they're willing to say "yes" to almost anything.

I have heard so many directors' horror stories. Sometimes they had a terrible line producer or producer who didn't maintain the "production bible" properly, and contracts and deal memos were missing, or hadn't been signed at all. Directors whose producers have long since moved on to another project, and they are left trying to figure out how to negotiate an offer without knowing what they deserve, what they want, or what's even possible for their project. The director wants to be wanted, to know her film will reach audiences, and knows that distribution is key for future film financing. This puts filmmakers in a vulnerable position, keen to say "yes" to an offer.

I call this the you-don't-know-what-you-don't-know problem. There are things you know that you don't know. For example, I know that I don't know how to ride a motorcycle.

But I didn't know that I didn't know that in the United States, pretty much anyone can pursue a lawsuit against you. They can do this even if they don't have evidence to support their lawsuit, because they don't need that until summary judgment or trial, which could be months or years down the road, and this process costs you money to defend yourself. In the meantime, you need to continue to address their lies until you are in court and able to prove the allegations are untrue, or you reach an out-of-court settlement to make it all go away.

I had to waste my time doing the latter, and furthermore, I had to walk away being owed thousands of dollars. Ultimately, it was worth it because A) I never have to talk to this person again, and B) I learned how important contractual law is in such circumstances.

Think about it: someone has a nervous breakdown during your work together and decides they want to sue you for reasons that are untrue. Doesn't matter. They can file their lawsuit based on nonsense if they have the energy and skill to do it themselves, or they find a lawyer who is willing to help them. And you are in a position where you have to defend yourself, regardless of whether they have supporting evidence or not.

Now think about this: you have worked for years on your project, from script to screen, and you have been offered a distribution deal. If you don't know what you don't know, you will not ask for all the things to which you and your project are entitled.

Clearly, this chapter is THE foundation of your contractual law education. Distribution is the place where most artists find themselves prone on the floor, wishing they were dead... or their producer was. It is where you realize all the mistakes you made in the beginning. A full understanding of what distribution possibilities are available for you and your project before you begin production is the best gift you can give yourself.

Now, I could go on and on about how many bottles of vodka and cartons of cigarettes I've gone through just to write this book, but let me be clear: This particular chapter will have Orly Ravid written all over it.

She has championed artists in the distribution arena for over 2 decades – long before she was a lawyer. From her own consultancy business and working at Wolfe Releasing and Senator Entertainment, to founding and running The Film Collaborative, and to her current position as a lawyer at Mitchell Silberberg & Knupp LLP, Orly will not let you take a less-than-pristine distribution deal if she can help it. Much of the information that follows is based on an interview I did with Orly in person, and a keynote talk she gave at a film event.

If I meet you at a cocktail party, and you tell me you read this book, and you follow that up with you got screwed in distribution based on contractual ineffectiveness, I will know you didn't really read this chapter.

Let us proceed, my friend.

WHERE IS THE PAPERWORK YOU NEED?

You may be in a position of having to spend thousands of dollars up front because you didn't have the right SAG-AFTRA contracts in place, or you don't know to insist on a Distributor's Assumption Agreement (one that declares that the distributor will assume the cost of any residuals out of the money they're making on the film, otherwise you will be on the hook for those fees in perpetuity). SAGindie's Darrien Gipson breaks it down for us:

> "The biggest issue is that the filmmaker doesn't understand how to protect themselves when the film is finished and somebody is actually interested in distributing their film. SAG-AFTRA has always included a Distributor's Assumption Agreement in all the paperwork. Which means that if Company B says, 'Roberta, I want your film, and I'm going to distribute it throughout the US and go to some foreign markets, etc.,' your job, or your attorney's job, is to say, 'Company B, great! And here is the SAG-AFTRA Distributor's Assumption Agreement for you to sign.' The Assumption says that every single time Company B sells your film anywhere, and it creates a residual amount to be owed to the talent in your film, that Company B will pay the residuals out of the money they're making on the film. If you do not have them do it, then when they say, 'I want to distribute your film, and hey here's $100,000 for your film,' or however much, and then they sell it all over the US, and HBO, Starz, whatever, then there's a $30,000 residual fee that's now owed and that bill is going to come to YOU, because you're the producer on record and you're the one who's legally assuming it because Company

B didn't sign the Assumption Agreement. Then they get to Cannes and they sell it to Spanish cable, that's another $50,000 bill that's going to come to you. And it's going to keep going, every time they package it, sell it, move it, do anything to it, in perpetuity, you're going to keep getting bills forever."

Good Lord. Ain't nobody got time for that.

Michelle Mower experienced this firsthand. She shares:

"One of the most frustrating things to deal with as a first-time filmmaker is the Distributor Assumption Agreement. The company I signed with was a sales agency, not a distributor, but they sold the film to distributors. None, and I mean NONE, of them would sign the assumption agreement. I had no idea that if they didn't sign it, I was liable to pay thousands of dollars in residuals every single time they sold the film! It was an expensive lesson to learn but in the end the residuals were paid, and we were even able to help a few local actors become SAG eligible."

You might be thinking, "Well, I wouldn't make that mistake. I read all the documents I sign and would remember this clause needs to be in my distribution deal." But will you?

Something to note is that many smaller independent distribution companies will simply not take on any union obligations, so be mindful of that in evaluating the deal and the financial reality of your distribution situation overall. If you are required to pay the actor residuals, make sure the deal you're signing makes financial sense to your bottom line.

WHEN IT COMES TO DISTRIBUTION, THE LAW CAN BE USELESS

Orly often says when it comes to distribution, "the law can be useless." She continues:

> "Not literally, of course, but effectively, because having a lawyer negotiate and draft or redline your contract focusing on the legal provisions is just half the battle. It may be useless if the deal should not be entered into in the first place, because it is so bad that it does not matter what your rights to sue them are. The contract's basic business terms suck and you've signed up for them.

> "Filmmakers blindly give over their rights and/or copyright using a lawyer who does not thoroughly understand distribution. I would argue that some entertainment lawyers do not thoroughly understand distribution, or what can be done in terms of the best exploitation of rights for best fees and possible costs recouped.

> "Really, you're looking to hire a lawyer at this stage based on their skills in distribution – not just one who understands actor deal memos, production legal, or copyright issues such as fair use. Sometimes you will have one lawyer who can really do it all or you may have two lawyers handling your film's needs based on their individual legal focus. That's okay. Better that than make mistakes."

YOU ONLY HAVE THE RIGHTS THAT ARE IN YOUR CONTRACT

I know producers, myself included, who have signed work-for-hire deals that ended up being the worst decision they could have made. The deal memo didn't speak to the future. The "what ifs." What if a producer pours their blood, sweat, and tears into a small project that becomes a much larger one? You produce the half-hour pilot for less than $100k, and the director who hired you gets offered a deal to create a series. What claims do you have to either be involved with producing the series, or at the very least, continue to be named as the producer? You are only getting what is in your contract. Nothing more, nothing less (hopefully). The pilot that is now a television series? You are not entitled to be part of this new deal because you signed a contract saying you released your rights.

Effie T. Brown describes her experience when she realized she was not contractually attached to a television series on a film she produced, despite an MFN clause among all the producers (some of whom *were* attached):

> "I got rid of that old lawyer and got a new, fancy, high-powered lawyer who says, 'You totally have a case, I'm looking at it right here.' Meanwhile, I got my television executive job, so it took the bitterness off of it. Then, my new fancy lawyer says, 'It switched. You're never going to win it, because it says in your contract that you cannot be a part of a series if you are an executive at another television company or studio.' It does, it actually says that. At the time, it was the furthest thing from my mind. I was gagging to get into television; that's why I was doing this

million-dollar movie with two weeks of prep, because I was trying to get in. The only reason I could think of why I was being cut out despite the MFN is because I was a dick. I was effective on the movie, but I didn't do it in a way that I guess made everybody feel good, or feel like they wanted me to be a part of future things. That's where the worst thing that could happen has happened: They started production the day before yesterday, and they're giving me nothing.

"I do remember the lawyer bringing up that clause, and I thought, 'Should I be so lucky to have that problem!' Guess what? This is what the lucky problem looks like. But that was where it fell apart contractually. Those were the bullets in the gun that was used against me. Truly, the spirit behind those bullets was that I was difficult. I made it harder than it should have been for the people that matter. This is where I fucked up, and this is where a piece of paper never circumvents relationships. *Relationships, in my opinion, will always trump a contract.* This is a big life lesson: To know when to walk away, and to know when you can be right, or you can be happy. You have to also play the long game. Stop fighting. Stop fighting and focus on what you got, not what you got screwed out of."

It's a terrible reality for many producers that happens all of the time. See Chapter 1 for a list of possibilities that you could include in your contract as a producer or director for hire.

Shelby Stone, the President of Production for Freedom Road Productions, offers advice on how to get this in your work-for-hire agreement:

"Do I have the right of first refusal on a sequel, should there be a sequel? Or prequel? Do I have any rights if it's turned into a TV series, theatrical, or Broadway piece? Rights holders, depending on the material, will negotiate these issues, but some will not. The DGA has its own rules which are worth examining even if you're not DGA yet. Conversely, a your attorney can and should claim that without your directorial vision, they wouldn't be clamoring for a prequel or sequel, and that's where the negotiation conversation has to go."

Orly illustrates below for us what can happen when we sign a contract not knowing what we didn't know:

"You only have the rights that are in your contract, so before you enter into a contract think through – does the deal make sense? And then ask yourself, 'How can the deal terms be better for you?' Remember, the business terms may matter more than the legal ones. If you can think of it, put it in your contract. This includes things that are important to you such as festival runs, festival travel, marketing, publicity, Academy qualifying, awards campaigns generally, credits, prize money, release scope, release timing, and cross-promotions.

"Have a meaningful conversation with your potential distributor about what is important to you and why – fully understand their entire plan. You also need to get real about your potential and negotiation leverage. I cover more about that below."

ORLY'S RED FLAG CHEAT SHEET

I hate to use a cliché but the devil is in the details: People glaze over boilerplate fine print, Standard Terms and Conditions, and definitions, but that is often the language that dictates how good the deal is. If you're trying to evaluate a contract at first glance here are some things to think about:

CONTRACT LENGTH: TOO SHORT OR REALLY LONG

You might think a contract's length is unimportant. Orly shares her thoughts:

> "**Too short:** When a contract is just 2 or a few pages it may look innocent, and the sender may have the best of intentions, but keep in mind it is very likely some things aren't covered. And if the sender does not have the best of intentions, and practices, you need to work through the issues rather than risking ambiguity/conflict.

> "Many European distributors use shorter contracts and one wants to balance protecting oneself from being too onerous and alienating a good company and killing a good deal. Again, that's why working with an attorney who knows the distribution landscape is key.

> "**Really Long (15-40 pages):** This is where you need to pay attention to every clause and every definition! Studio deals and most bigger distribution companies have longer long forms that require careful reading."

DEFINITIONS: GROSS RECEIPTS VS. NET RECEIPTS

Orly elaborates on two key definitions you should look out for:

"As far as the definitions go, it doesn't really matter what the plain language words mean to you if there's an explicit definition in the contract. It should be noted that in a case of dispute, if a term is not defined specifically, then the plain language would be interpreted normally, unless industry trade terms are used, in which case they would be interpreted accordingly. You must know what terms are defined and what those definitions mean. You should also make sure any term that matters is clearly defined. One key example of this is the definition of Gross Receipts and Net Receipts. Gross Receipts sounds like, and often is, all the money received at source with no deductions, but there are many instances where Gross Receipts is defined to allow for all sorts of deductions. Net Receipts is another definition you want to understand intimately – what exactly is being deducted (recouped). And you'll want to cap that (meaning limit it).

"For example: Filmmaker does a deal with Distributor whereby Filmmaker is getting 70% of "Gross Receipts," but actually, in the contract, "Gross Receipts" is defined not as all money received from first dollar from all sources without deductions, but it is defined as the money received by Distributor LESS certain marketing fees or overhead expenses or who knows what…

"Another thing to look out for is where Gross Receipts is defined as all the money that Distributor gets, but Distributor does all its sales or most of them through another entity that it owns, and that entity takes a fee before Distributor even gets any money. See how your Gross Receipts pie can get eaten up?

"Yet another common issue is where Distributor takes a Distribution Fee from Gross Receipts (which then is likely defined as including no deductions, but just being all the revenue period). But, Filmmaker is actually only getting a percentage left over after Distributor gets yet another piece of the pie: its share of Back End Revenue, after all expenses are recouped. So let's say Gross Revenue was $100,000 and the Distribution Fee was 30% to Distributor, expenses were $15,000 (fully recoupable), and the Back End Revenue was split 50/50 between Distributor and Filmmaker.

"The math waterfall works out like this:
$100,000 Gross Revenue
− $30,000 Distribution Fee
− $15,000 Recoupable Expenses
$55,000 to be split 50/50

"In this scenario, Filmmaker only gets $27,500 out of $100,000 in Gross Revenue."

MIDDLEMEN

Orly warns against distributors who utilize middlemen instead of doing the work directly:

"Know what the distributor is doing directly versus what they need to distribute through middlemen. For example, some distributors take all digital rights but then rely on another company (an aggregator/middleman) to distribute those rights to various digital platforms. Why does this matter? Because another fee will be taken out, and so the Gross Receipts to your distributor is not what the platform remitted, but what the platform remitted less another company's distribution fee and maybe additional expenses too. It is the same issue for educational distribution, foreign sales, and licensing in general. Another trick I have seen a distributor do is funnel direct-to-consumer sales through a separate company the distributor owns, such that another fee is deducted. Meanwhile, this distributor's value stemmed from the direct-sales potential, but now you've paid two distribution fees for the sale. Get clear and get that clarity in writing."

COMMITMENTS AND MERGER CLAUSE

Orly shares the importance of getting promises in writing in your final contract:

"Filmmakers often choose which distributor to go with based on a marketing vision and the distributor's release promises. Get those in writing because your contract will almost certainly have what is called a 'merger clause,' AKA 'integration clause,' that provides that nothing said orally or even in writing before the contract matters. In other words, if it's not in the contract, it may not happen. So get in writing any release patterns and marketing you have been promised."

TERMINATION PROVISION

It may be wise to pursue this provision according to Orly:

"Get a termination provision that allows for termination of the contract in case of uncured material breach. It is rare to find such a provision permitting you to terminate, but try to get it. Proceed carefully if the distributor won't allow it. A distributor should allow such a provision provided they have an opportunity to cure material breach upon 30 days' notice."

ALL RIGHTS DEALS

It is important to be aware of which rights a distributor in capable of exploiting in Orly's experience:

"Don't give a distributor rights that it is not well-positioned and experienced in exploiting. You may then be stuck with no one properly exploiting those rights and you won't be able to either. Reserve those rights so either another company can work with them or you can via DIY. Similarly, try to keep your term on the deal short, and mutually agree to extend if things are going well – but no need to enter into a long term only to be stuck."

Ondi Timoner, two-time Sundance Grand Jury prize winner, explains her strategy:

"The middleman is not gone, but can be of great assistance. They've changed what hats they wear, and those who are smart have adjusted the way that they present to us, but there's no longer the gatekeeper in that way. You can reach your fans and there are all sorts of ways to do it, there are ways to have your own store, and think about all that stuff.

"When you're making distribution deals you need to make sure that you have the underlying rights to all your footage, and you have the rights to put out extras if you want, or merchandise if you want. Make short distribution deals now. With *We Live in Public*, we made a two-year internet distribution deal, and right there, two years later, they had either given us the profits or they hadn't. They had either reported honestly or they hadn't. If they wanted to keep the title, they were accountable. Enough with the 15-year windows. Forget it. Don't even do that. If they really want your movie, they'll play ball, you know? These days, it's just inappropriate."

Shelby Stone adds her take on the rapid development in technology:

"These days, you and your lawyer have to think about new technologies that we don't know about yet. Remember, nobody made deals to participate in streaming. No one knew there was going to be streaming. Now with the rise of virtual reality, you have to think about that. What if they make some part of the film a virtual reality experience, do you participate in that? You just have to keep your eye on the basics, and think about the future."

ASSIGNMENT PROVISION

Orly warns against allowing assignment provisions without tailoring them:

"An assignment provision means that the Distributor (or whichever party has assignment rights) can basically give the rights that party has in the contract to another party. So if the Distributor has the right to assign the contract with you, then that means that one day you may find out another company is handling your distribution. I try to limit the distributor's ability to assign the contract or the rights and recommend you do the same.

"At the very least, try to make sure you can approve in advance, that the terms and conditions of your agreement would be honored, and that the company assigning the rights is secondarily liable. It is common and acceptable that a distributor (or any company) would want the right to assign the rights should that company be bought out, but still insist on the suggested protections. This does not always become an issue, but if an executive at a company is the reason you are doing the deal (based on that executive's vision and capacity to handle your film well) and then all of a sudden that company assigns the rights to another company – well you can see why that may not work out well for you."

BANKRUPTCY/INSOLVENCY

What if your distributor goes out of business? Orly explains:

"I recommend you insist on a provision (if it is not there and if you cannot terminate any time) to get your rights back if the distributor becomes insolvent or files for bankruptcy. Otherwise, you may be stuck with your rights tied up but no revenue (and maybe no activity even) for your film."

Ondi Timoner's film *DIG!* is tied up due to just such complications:

"I made my distribution deal for *DIG!* just hours before I won the Grand Jury Prize. And that was under a lot of pressure from the sales agent who, understandably, wanted to make sure we locked in something great in case I didn't win. Somehow I was blind to the fact that I was going to win, so I went ahead and took his advice.

Another thing that happened as a result of that deal was, first of all, I went with a distributor that is now basically defunct. And nobody who made a deal with that distributor can get their movies back for years on end now. That distribution company, Palm Pictures, every filmmaker that you talk to from Palm wants their rights back. I've even offered to split everything 50/50 with them if I could just please have the right to make this available to the public. *DIG!* is a very popular title."

RESIDUALS

Get clear on who is assuming responsibility for the residuals. Orly agrees:

"As Roberta mentions above, if you have SAG-AFTRA obligations, get clear on who is assuming those residual obligations. Studios generally assume them, but smaller indie distributors often do not. Have a clear understanding of what it may cost you in the long run if the distributor does not assume this responsibility – which actors will get how much money in each category of distribution, and what levels of success, etc."

COPYRIGHT RIGHTS

Orly explains what a mortgage of copyright and when a distributor might ask for it:

"Distributors will often want a mortgage of copyright. The reason sometimes stated is that the distributor needs a lien in case the producers fail to pay union dues, or any other obligations, and then the distributor needs that mortgage of copyright as a lien in case it has to pay those obligations in order to continue distributing the film. I almost always get rid of that provision, or at least tailor it, because there is no reason for you to just give up the copyright to your film to a distributor if you can help it. A mortgage of copyright is standard only where the distributor is at risk of being in a lending position to your film. This is unavoidable sometimes where the distributor is paying your residuals and wants the copyright as security interest to protect itself given those residuals obligations."

CHOICE OF VENUE

Choice of venue can be key, as Orly notes below:

"Choice of Venue simply means the parties are deciding where a dispute should be resolved should one take place; e.g. courts in Los Angeles County in the State of California. One wants to select a venue where one resides. Contract law is governed by state law (whereas Copyright law is federal). CA and NY law are quite similar, though not exactly the same, and there are a few key differences (such as when evidence extraneous to the contract itself is admissible in court; NY has a stricter standard). It is probably wise to have a lawyer who practices law in the state that is the governing law of the contract."

Usually, a company won't permit changing this because that would obviously be very inconvenient. However, sometimes, where a company is in Europe or the Middle East and the other party is in California, the parties might agree to New York City as a venue (a happy middle ground).

ARBITRATION VS. LITIGATION VS. MEDIATION

Orly describes the pros and cons of each option:

> "You won't often have the flexibility to choose how a dispute should be handled, should one arise, but know what these provisions amount to and think through what is better for you when you have a choice.

> "**Arbitration:** Not in court, not public, before a private arbitrator or panel of 3 arbitrators in an arbitration forum such as ADR, JAMS, AAA, IFTA. Pros – cheaper, private, not public record, more controllable, arbitrator will be familiar with distribution, more efficient. Cons – Arbitrator may be favorable to distributor, no threat of public litigation, risk of embarrassment or loss of business, which may be a motivator.

> "**Litigation:** In court, public, before a judge or jury. Pros – can be used as a threat against a company who doesn't want bad publicity. Cons – expensive, time-consuming, may damage filmmaker's relationships and reputation.

> "**Mediation:** Private, not free, but often cheaper than litigation. The softest option, friendliest, and can be functional.

> "**Small Claims:** In court, public, before a judge. I like to build in a provision to go to Small Claims court, which is more affordable and practical for indie filmmakers than either arbitration or litigation, but there's a cap on the amount you can sue for. No lawyers can be with you, and damages are limited to a sum such as $10,000, depending on the state law."

WHO ARE YOU IN THE FOOD CHAIN?

Orly describes the importance of setting goals early and understanding your negotiation leverage:

> "It's important to know who you are in the food chain, and it's important to resolve the possibly varying objectives of the people who own and control the project. For example, directors may care less about paying back investors and more about having a bigger release (even if less financially sustainable) in an effort to elevate their profile and increase the potential of financing their next project and/or being hired to direct another film or TV series. Producers may care more about wanting to recoup and pay investors back, so that they can go back to those investors for the next project. In any case, I recommend defining your goals at the outset and contracting accordingly. Also, if you're making a documentary, maybe (likely) changing the world is more important than money, and so you may opt for a distribution scenario that is less financially sustainable but will ultimately affect greater reach and increased likelihood of impact. Whatever your objectives, apart from getting clear from the start, be realistic about your film's potential (research comps) so that you're all operating from a realistic foundation of knowledge and assumptions.

> "It's easy for me to toss out all that you should watch out for and try to get in any licensing or distribution deal, but not all films or filmmakers have the same negotiation leverage. In terms of negotiation leverage, factors to keep in mind are, in no particular order: (1) the fame of director and talent in the film (producer too, but often

less so), (2) pedigree of premieres (which festivals), (3) publicity, (4) social media capital, (5) targetable niche, and (6) popularity/buzz in general."

SALES AGENTS, DISTRIBUTORS, AGGREGATORS, AND PLATFORMS: WHAT'S IN A NAME?

Knowing the difference between these company and service types will help you make smart decisions. Orly elaborates:

> "One source of confusion I find is the conflation of various company and service types. Filmmakers confuse sales agents, distributors, aggregators, and platforms. That's why below I define them as a guideline to help you determine what distribution fees are appropriate based on what the company is actually doing and offering (regardless of what it calls itself). By conflating these different service types you end up confusing your expectations of them, and ultimately doing a bad deal. So, while this may seem a bit granular in distribution, understanding this will help you better understand what to ask for in a contract and what not to sign.

> "**Sales Agent:** A person or company representing your rights to other distributors and buyers. Sales agents take a commission for the sale that should not be greater than 10% for domestic (US/Canada sales), but can go lower depending on how big the sale is. However, European and World sales agents take 15% minimum (rare), but more often than not take 25 - 35%. The key is to know which sales agents make sense for your film, and also the potential sales, so you know how much you are paying in commission. Sales agents can be helpful, but are not a

panacea, so don't give away a commission if you can do the sales yourself (though most filmmakers cannot). Importantly, there are lots of crooks out there, so be careful and always address recoupable expenses. Another key is to get clear as to whether the commission is of the minimum guarantee/license fee or from all revenues in connection with the deal. Usually it's the latter, though not always. Is the deal between producers and the buyer, or via the sales agent's company? You can guess which I prefer (though that puts the onus of collections on you).

"**Distributor**: Companies that release your film in theaters, festivals, educational, DVD, and digital will want your rights for a set number of years or in perpetuity, and often take all your rights. The key is the company should do more than just plop your film onto a digital platform. The distributor should make some sort of marketing commitment and display some skill in distribution. Distributors take usually at least 20% and often as much as 35% or more in distribution fees (commission). Again, keep in mind overall revenue potential and what fees are taken for which category of distribution. It varies and depends on the work required and whether expenses are recouped or not.

"**Aggregator**: A service that gets your film onto platforms for a smaller commission (15% or 20% max) or modest flat fee, for a much shorter term than a Distributor (only 2-3 years), though is usually not providing any marketing or publicity.

"**Platform**: A digital storefront such as Amazon, iTunes, Netflix, Hulu, Google Play, etc. One can sell directly to

Netflix and Amazon for a fee for 2 or 3 years (like a TV license), for example, or directly through a sales agent, though most often one will still have to deliver through an approved aggregator or distributor.

"I recommend doing a math waterfall to understand how much money will be coming your way at the end of the day, and not obsessing over the commission so much as what the agent/distributor can do for you vs. what you can do or want to do yourself, and what that looks like in the overall analysis. Ask for projections and what they think the key revenue streams and interest exposure are for the film, and do your own homework to vet accordingly."

ORLY'S CONTRACTS 101:
SOME GENERAL TIPS AND NOTES

- If your lawyer makes a mistake, they will have to fix it, and their liability insurance will cover damages if they don't and if they committed malpractice (assuming you sue in time and prove legal malpractice which is a tall burden but still... an option). Without a lawyer, for sure only YOU will be liable.
- Always hire a lawyer if you're doing a deal bigger than you've ever negotiated successfully.
- Incorporate yourself as soon as you have anything to lose, to protect your personal property.
- Some free legal resources in California: Southwestern Legal Clinic, California Voice for the Arts, TFC Legal (coming soon)

- Distributors are not often going to be sending you a contract with best-case-scenario terms. See that first draft as such: a draft.

- Oral contracts can be binding in CA and NY, but don't rely on it: There is a two-year statute of limitations in CA from the date of the breach, and the statute of frauds prevents oral contracts from being valid if the agreement involves performance after a year. With oral contracts you always have difficulty proving what was agreed to. GET IT IN WRITING.

- Get contracts going, or at least deal memos, right away in the creative process, as soon as you want to rely on the project.

- Add a Performance Clause: If they don't reach a certain benchmark of performance, the rights revert back within a reasonable period of time that your film actually still has a life. That period may be different for domestic distribution than for international. Note that you won't always have the leverage to negotiate a performance clause – and be mindful because aggressive negotiations can be a business killer.

- Think about the bigger picture: focus not just on rights, but also on revenue levels. Consider including a provision or addendum that will cover you if there are changes in the industry (like the development of digital and online distribution).

- Waiver of Injunctive Relief provision: If you are waiving your right to injunctive (equitable) relief, that means that you are giving up your right to have things stop while a court analyzes your rights under the contract. If you are signing a contract with a distributor, you would want injunctive (equitable) relief if you want the distribution to stop, if you wanted your film back. However, you will want to be careful about giving such relief to people you hire, like talent or co-producers.

- Approval/Meaningful Consultation: If you have leverage, you'll want this on the release pattern and marketing.

ORLY'S TOP DEAL TERMS TO LOOK OUT FOR

- Minimum Guarantee: try to get a guarantee that you will at be paid that sum by a certain time (i.e. as soon as possible). Include a provision that the filmmaker will be paid on signing, on delivery, and on release or 90 days after release.
- Always examine the definitions of terms and expenses. All expenses must be approved and capped. Recoupable expenses should be only third party, outside expenses, not in-house or overhead. Don't allow cross-collateralization with other films. Don't allow a distributor/sales agent to license your film in a deal with other films, and allocate a sales price as it sees fit. Don't let the distributor/sales agent recoup expenses related to other films.
- If Distributor is getting a distribution fee, then fight if they are taking an additional share of the backend, especially if Distributor did not pay a lot for or toward the distribution.
- You should keep festival prize money if you can.
- Get audit rights, and get clear on when/how you can audit. Make sure you have at least 1-2 years after the end of the Term. If auditing reveals the distributor is significantly off in accounting, the distributor should pay for the auditor.

- Get your rights back, immediately, upon insolvency or bankruptcy.

A sample of an all-rights distribution agreement between producer and distributor, complete with annotations by Orly Ravid, can be found in the Appendix of this book.

6

It's Always a Good Time
to Make Magic

ROBERTA

I know. It's a ton of information. All we artists want is to just get out there and do it, goddamn it!

I feel you.

As I wrote this book, I often felt like I do when I'm writing a script: I have to believe that someone is holding a gun to my head to keep the writing flow going. It's hard. Writing is hard. Making films is even harder. But you know what is even harder than that?

Getting sued, or needing to sue the other side.

I've been through both, and I can tell you that from both sides - it sucks.

All that hard work you went through in the trenches of filmmaking swallowed up by bullshit.

So, here in these final pages I want to share some of my story with the hope that it helps move you forward in the direction of your dreams with this "ton of information."

Like many producers before me (as Effie notes earlier in her generously shared story), I ended up saying "yes" to a situation I should have said "no" to, and didn't realize the falsity of the *relationship* I was getting into with the director.

I worked harder than I had ever worked on a film, and unbeknownst to me, the director had a long list of people they had betrayed long before they'd met me. There were red flags, but I made excuses, or flat out ignored them. I had a great contract with this director, but not being one for details, I ended up executing the wrong one, which ultimately added to the possibility of them launching a lawsuit against me.

This was *after* the film was done. This was *after* I had gotten us into top tier film festivals. This was *after* I'd spent 2 years working all the magic I had to make it happen.

Was I mad? Sure. Angry? Sometimes. Sad? More often that I care to remember.

However, when it's all said and done, those *feelings* are fleeting and were easy to let go of. What I hope I never let go of is what I learned the hard way.

And it's what I hope *you* learn the easy way:

Success really is all about relationships.

A well-crafted contract will provide all parties with a sense of safety, but a well-developed relationship will provide you with much more than that. It will give you something to fall back on when things get hard (and they *always* get hard). A well-developed and respectful relationship will give you and your colleagues the ability to communicate when the going gets tough and all you want to do is walk away - or worse, all you want to do is sue them.

So please do spend time understanding and following all our advice in this book. It's fantastic advice. However, spend more time making sure that the *people* you're saying "yes" to are worth your time, energy, and hard work.

You take all that time with the script, with the hiring of the crew, the casting of the film, the seemingly endless post production, the marketing and distribution! So please, from the beginning, take the time to choose your colleagues wisely. Google and watch Ava Duvernay talking about being a "desperate filmmaker" in a fantastic keynote speech she gave at a forum for Film Independent in 2013. My friend, there is <u>no</u> room for desperation in your psyche. Because you know what desperation leads to?

Bad decisions. Saying "yes," when all your ass should be saying is "no."

I promise you, building fundamentally respectful, conscious relationships filled with great communication <u>alongside </u>that rock star contract is what is going to take you to the next level.

You have my word.

ORLY

I'm really not trying to sound like a grandmother before I even have my first child, but when I first started in international sales and distribution there were 35mm film prints (and negatives), VHS that sold to rental stores for $99 or more dollars, and then DVDs that generated even more revenue (though usually sold for less to rent). People collected VHS and DVDs. Costs added up because remember, before email, there was only FedEx for shipping ads, poster artwork, and film prints.

Deals were sometimes done on napkins, on yachts in Cannes, and movies were financed or sold based on a few decent attachments, a good genre, and a trailer. Now, post the indie film boom of the 1990s and early 2000s, the rise of new media and a multiplatform worldwide web, the marketplace is glutted, sales prices are low, and it's much more of a buyer's market.

That may sound like bad news but here's the upside: Before, one really could not finance a film or sell or distribute it without the middlemen, and now one can (crowdfunding, grants, the filmmaker brand/store, DIY distribution). And the costs have gone way, way down. With the changes in both costs and revenue, deal terms have sometimes changed, and where some are not current with the times, they ought to be. It used to be that Home Video distribution fees were very high (e.g. 75%) because of the costs and time/work involved in that type of distribution, whereas the fees for broadcast deals were lower (e.g. 30% or 40%) because all that involved was a licensing deal and relatively simple delivery. Now, TV and Internet are conflating (e.g. Netflix and Amazon). Domestic and International distribution are conflating (Netflix, based in the U.S., buys for the world; other digital platforms are trying to compete, and worldwide platforms reach out to filmmakers worldwide; iTunes, also US-based, is worldwide).

Bottom line: distribution has changed. You can achieve a lot without many middlemen, but whether or not you work with sales agents and distributors, think about the reality of the release campaign, costs, impact of those expenses, and revenue potential. Do the math. Ask around about what is fair and what is doable given what you are getting from the company/service. Understand what can be done. If a distributor wants to take 30% to do the same work an aggregator will do for 15% or a small flat fee, maybe go with the aggregator. I always like to do 'Fun with Math' waterfall charts with my clients because knowledge is power – don't hide from the reality of what you want both for your filmmaking career and your purse (whether to pay back investors so they will invest again or to pay yourself or your relatives back).

When you get real and get wise you can make meaningful decisions about your film and your path, and be fair to yourself, your crew, and the companies you work with. If you lay the groundwork, you may well establish a network of companies or a DIY system to work with for all your films. So please, don't hide from the knowledge: embrace it and let it work for you. And then, also remember to know what you don't know, and find out.

MICHELLE

Filmmaking is not for the faint of heart. It's hard as hell. It's also a very risky endeavor if you don't know what you are doing. Many first-time filmmakers think just because they know how to use a camera, they've learned all they need to learn to succeed in the film industry.

The fact is you need to understand the business of film just as much as you need to know how to use a camera, or else you'll end up getting sued or taken advantage of. But if you are open to learning how the industry works from development through distribution, you will have an edge amongst your filmmaking peers.

You will know what they don't know... how to make a career out of making movies.

Epilogue

Finding an Entertainment Lawyer

When it comes to entertainment law, there are boutique firms that actors and directors often use, because those firms work on a percentage of revenue (and if something comes up beyond the scope of that firm's legal practice, the firm or the client's manager can help the attorney seek additional legal counsel). Otherwise, producers/filmmakers go to smaller or larger law firms, or just solo practitioners. As we have already discussed, one should never just have a an attorney who does not practice entertainment law handle an entertainment agreement. That would be like having a pediatrician perform open heart surgery.

And the reasoning behind that extends even to selecting an entertainment attorney based on experience. For example, some lawyers do a lot more production legal, and if that is what you are looking for, go with an attorney who does that all day every day (and for a good price).

The same logic applies for, let's say, a fair use opinion (see brief fair use discussion in Chapter 1. If one's business involves entertainment and a lot of other potential matters, you may want to have a mid-size to bigger firm handle one's work to cover all the various issues and legal disciplines that come up – for example, having a work-for-hire provision in a writer agreement can trigger employment law issues in a state such as California.

Separately, in producing a film, issues may come up with respect to company formation (e.g. single purpose LLC), such as investor agreements that may trigger securities law issues.

So, one should think through the legal needs and find a legal practice capable of aptly handling all legal issues that may arise in getting you the end result. Additionally, not every entertainment attorney is as up-to-speed about distribution. Therefore, for those deals, find an attorney who is completely current and savvy that way. Ideally, you can have all your needs met via one or two firms max – depending on the complexity of your legal needs (and likely whether the lawyers practice out of New York or Los Angeles). Lastly, and this may seem obvious, but make sure your lawyer is actually licensed to practice law.

Appendix

Sample Annotated Contract

Sample All-Rights Distribution Agreement Between Producer and Distributor.

[This agreement was sourced on the Internet by Orly Ravid so as not to breach the confidence of any clients or parties to a deal. Although it's a distribution agreement, some provisions would be found in any agreement. Please also recall the disclaimer at the beginning of this book. Annotations are written by Orly Ravid and are bracketed and in bold text.]

XXX DISTRIBUTOR DISTRIBUTION RIGHTS AGREEMENT

This Distribution Rights Agreement (the "Agreement") is effective as of [Month], [Day], 20XX (the "Effective Date"), by and between XXX ("Distributor"), and YYY Productions, ("Licensor"), with regard to the motion picture entitled "ABC" (the "Picture").

1.   <u>GRANTED RIGHTS</u>:

(a)   Licensor hereby exclusively and irrevocably (subject to the terms and conditions herein) grants to Distributor throughout the License Period (as defined below) and the Licensed Territory (as defined below) all distribution and exploitation rights of every kind in and relating to the Picture including, without limitation, the sole and exclusive right, license and privilege under copyright to, and to authorize, license and sublicense others to exhibit, distribute, transmit, reproduce, manufacture, publicly display, project, publicly perform, advertise, promote and otherwise exploit the Picture (including clip and footage licenses related to the Picture) in any and all media or medium, now or hereafter devised, by all means of transmission and delivery, now known or hereafter devised, in all languages, and in all versions, including, without limitation, all forms of theatrical and non-theatrical exhibition, ancillary exhibition (e.g., airlines, ships and military bases), all forms of home video (including but not limited to electronic sell through and rental, videocassettes, DVDs and CD-ROMs), all forms of television exhibition (including but not limited to free television, basic and pay cable, pay per view, and all forms of on-demand), and all means of digital exhibition including without limitation broadband, mobile, internet streaming, and on-line transmission and delivery (collectively, the "Granted Rights"). The parties agree that the Granted Rights shall include the right to advertise and promote the Picture in the Licensed Territory (and if the Licensed Territory hereunder is not worldwide, then non-exclusively worldwide with respect to advertising and promoting on the Internet, provided that any such Internet or on-line promotion, or promotion by similar technologies/mediums which are accessible outside the Licensed Territory, shall limit the display of clips and trailers of the Picture to no more than three (3) minutes in length) in any manner or media, now known or hereafter devised, including, without limitation, the right to use and license others to use Licensor's name and the title of, trailers created for and excerpts from the Picture (including audio portions only) and the name, voice and likeness of and any biographical material furnished by Licensor concerning all main cast and key crew (including the producers of the Picture) appearing in or connected with the Picture for the purpose of advertising, promoting and/or publicizing the Picture, the Distributor, the licensee, and/or the program service on which the Picture is exhibited, subject to any reasonable and customary third party contractual restrictions of which Licensor has notified Distributor in writing as part of Delivery (as defined in Paragraph 9(b) below). As between Licensor and Distributor, all rights of exploitation of the Picture which do not involve the distribution or exhibition of the Picture or excerpts thereof (the Reserved Rights"), including, without limitation, soundtrack album, music publishing, novelization or other publication rights are hereby reserved to Licensor. **[Whatever the agreement, always pay careful attention to any grant of rights, rights to control, and of course any other duties and obligations. This agreement concerns distribution and so rights are being granted from the production company (filmmakers / rights holders) to the distributor. Any time rights are being granted you'll want** to pay very careful attention to not include any rights you do not have to, nor include any rights that cannot be properly exploited per terms that make sense and that are the best you can get. You should very clearly and expressly reserve any and all rights that you do not intend to grant and that cannot be best exploited by the distributor (as opposed to yourself directly or via another company or service). Pay very careful attention to how rights are defined, especially if royalties and/or distribution fees vary. Recall that once upon a time no one believed that digital rights would be worth much but now they're critical. If you let those rights be included in a category such as home video rights where too big of a fee was taken out before you got your share you'd have been giving money away for no good reason, especially given the costs for digital distribution are much lower than that for traditional home video (physical media to brick and mortar stores). Also, wherever possible have the grant be "non-exclusive" though that is often not doable. At the very least have care-outs for self-distribution wherever possible. Also try to avoid the granting of rights being irrevocable. Instead, have rights revert back upon material breach, lack of performance based on certain benchmarks, that sort of setting of standards so that the grant is not without protections for you in case of, for example: lack of performance, bankruptcy, insolvency, the company no longer being in the field of film distribution, and of course uncured material breach.]

Distributor acknowledges that Licensor has employed a third party television sales agent for the purposes of television sales in the United States. Until the date that is three (3) months from the Effective Date of this Agreement (the "Television Sales Holdback"), Distributor shall not solicit television sales. Licensor agrees that it shall terminate effective the end of Television Sales Holdback, any and all third party television sales representation and that Distributor shall have the sole right to solicit and execute any television sales agreements. **[Always know which rights are being exploited directly, or not. If through middlemen (e.g. sub-distributors, theatrical bookers, other services), know what fees and expenses are being deducted and also know which companies. I try to avoid middlemen where possible but occasionally there is a good reason for going through one company and having it work through another for something specific (for example, the terms might be better or that middleman may not ever go direct with individual filmmakers.) Holdbacks are common but that is why it's critical to know and plan all licensing as part of an entire overall release strategy and license and release accordingly. Some films have higher probability of making money via one category of distribution over another which should also impact your analysis but this is more of a distribution / business strategy issue than legal one.]**

(b)   All sequel, prequel, remake and television production rights (e.g., episodic series, miniseries, and movies of the week) in connection with the Picture (each, a "Subsequent Production right") shall be retained by Licensor but shall be deemed "frozen" (i.e., may not be licensed or exploited) until three (3) years after the

U.S. Home Video release date. **[Always pay attention to any rights to underlying material and to any remake rights. "Frozen" means neither party can exploit. Ideally avoid this so you can exploit right away. But of course be mindful of these rights being included where you did not mean them to be and do not need them to be. They can be very valuable.]**

(c)   To effectuate the Granted Rights, Licensor shall execute concurrently herewith, the Instruction of Transfer attached as Exhibit A.

2.   <u>LICENSED TERRITORY</u>: Worldwide (the "Licensed Territory"). **[This is the parts of the world for which the rights are being granted. First of all, avoid the territory being defined as the "Universe" in case we do start inhabiting other planets. Second, of course limit this the same was you would the granted rights. Only studios have the capacity to properly handle worldwide rights. Best to split rights among the companies and services best-suited to monetize and promote them.]**

3.   <u>LICENSE PERIOD</u>: Commencing as of the Effective Date and continuing for seven (7) years from the Delivery (as defined in clause 9(b) (the "License Period"). **[This is the length of time that the rights are being granted. For aggregators term should be just 2 or 3 years where possible; 7 years is not unusual for distribution but of course companies like terms to be as long as possible, to beef up their libraries. It's always good to keep terms short and you can always renew if given a good reason. Also beware of automatic renewal provisions unless you provide notice to cancel – try to avoid because you will forget to prevent that in time. A sell-off period of 6 months after the end of the License Period (also referred to as "Term") was normal when VHS and then DVD was significant but there should be no need for that now.]**

4.   <u>PARTICIPATION IN NET RECEIPTS</u>:

(a)   Distributor agrees to pay to Licensor one hundred percent (100%) of Net Receipts. "Net Receipts" shall mean Gross Receipts after deduction for (i) payment to Distributor of the Distribution Fee as defined below in clauses 4.(a) 1-4; (iii) all costs and expenses incurred by Distributor in connection with the promotion, distribution and exploitation of the Picture, in any manner and media, including, without limitation, all manufacturing and packaging costs for HE Devices (as defined herein) (the "Distribution Expenses"). ~~If the Picture is licensed for distribution as part of a package or library including other programming (e.g., via subscription video on-demand), Distributor shall evaluate the Picture individually and allocate a share of gross receipts derived therefrom and the related expenses to the Picture as Distributor determines in its good faith judgment based on the fair market value or usage of the Picture, as the case may be.~~ **[I have crossed-out the language of the language just before this sentence (suggesting that it be rejected/omitted) because it leaves too much discretion for the distributor to sell your film in a package and** allocate pricing. You may choose to not permit your film to be sold in a package but you may have the type of film that sells well that way and is limited otherwise in which case instead of limiting those sales, just get approval rights over the deal or state you cannot get less than other films and only be sold with films of similar quality (though that is not so easy to define). Bottom line is: be mindful of this and handle appropriately for the benefit of your film. This sort of provision is not in every distribution agreement but pay attention to language that discusses cross-collateralizing revenues and selling your film in a package and do not allow it without knowing what you are getting yourself into and why.

Zooming out to broader issues: sometimes definitions of terms such as "Gross Receipts" and "Net Receipts" are buried in the "Standard Terms and Conditions" section of an agreement. Be sure to read and truly understand every single defined term, especially ones involving rights and money, duties and obligations on either side -- but read all terms. Here, Distribution Expenses should not only be very precisely defined (it is defined) but capped at a certain sum that should not be exceeded unless with written permission by you. Also, expenses must be actual and out-of-pocket and not cover in-house staff or overhead. So it matters who is doing marketing and publicity and theatrical booking and how those costs are being handled. If recoupable, you are essentially paying for them because the distributor will usually recoup all those expenses (and take its distribution fee) before remitting monies to you (unless you have some sort of gross corridor (money slice (e.g. 10%) to you off the top), which is hard to get and won't fully take of issues of overspending and recoupment).

In Option Purchase Agreements one deals with different terms ("Net Proceeds" and "Modified Adjusted Gross Receipts" a/k/a "MAGR") that address backend participation and there, whatever the terms are, one wants (whenever possible) to make sure the definitions will be clear and also that one will enjoy the same definition of net proceeds (or whatever it's being called) as anyone else in the best position to get backend.]

The "Distribution Fee" shall be an amount equal to: [As noted above, make sure all the rights are defined and that you know what percentage is beign given to you and taken out for each category and do a business analysis as well when evaluating and negotiating the deal.]

    1.   _35%_ with respect to all forms of theatrical and non-theatrical rights; [Appropriate but depends on overall theatrical deal]

    2.   _35%_ with respect to all forms of television rights; [Appropriate but careful with TV's conflict with SVOD (subscription video on demand)]

3.   _35%_ with respect to all forms of home video rights; **[Appropriate but could be lower and also about to be obsolete]**

4.   _35%_ with respect to all digital rights; **[Too high, try for 15%, 20%, or 25% depending on how much marketing and other work being done to earn fee]**

5.   _50%_ with respect to all ancillary rights; **[Could be appropriate; depends on rights, if any middlemen and overall release details and marketing]**

(b)   "Gross Receipts" shall mean one hundred percent (100%) of all non-refundable amounts actually received by or credited to Distributor from the exercise of the Granted Rights after deduction for all refunds, credits, discounts, allowances, rebates and set-offs, and a provision for reserves against returns and credits (which such reserves shall not exceed twenty-five percent (25%) of Home Video Device gross receipts, which shall be liquidated not less frequently than every twelve (12) months). [I try to limit the reserves, especially nowadays given the state of home video. Also, one wants to avoid the distributor incurring expenses in trying to sell big volume to brick and mortar stores such as WalMart only to have to pay for the costs of taking that inventory back. That could eat away at your revenues. Gross Receipts should be all monies from first dollar with no deductions and also make sure you have language that avoids a distributor treating their catalog or website, for example, as a separate company.]

5.   PAYMENT; ACCOUNTING: [Accounting should be no less than quarterly (though later into the term it can be bi-annual) if at all possible, ideally 30 days after the quarter though sometimes it will be 45 or 60. There should also be an Audit provision and your expenses for any audit should be covered if a material mistake is found indicating underpayment to you (this can be defined in dollars or percentages.)

(a)   Commencing with the first calendar quarter in which gross receipts in respect of the Picture are received by Distributor and on a quarterly basis for two years and, thereafter, on a semi-annual basis, Distributor shall furnish Licensor with a reasonably detailed statement showing the gross receipts, distribution expenses, calculation of Net Receipts, and the amount, if any, due to Licensor with respect to such period. Each statement shall be delivered to Licensor at the address listed in the first paragraph of this Agreement within sixty (60) days after the end of any applicable period in which Gross Receipts are received and shall be accompanied by payment of any amounts due to Licensor in U.S. dollars, subject to all laws and regulations requiring the deduction or withholding of payments for income or other taxes payable by or assessable against Licensor. All statements shall be deemed true and accurate and conclusively binding upon Licensor if not disputed by Licensor in writing within eighteen (18) months after the delivery of such statement and if a formal legal action is not commenced by Licensor within one year after such written objection. For the avoidance of doubt, if a formal legal action is commenced by Licensor, all statements to which such claim pertains shall not be deemed binding upon Licensor until such claim is resolved.

(b)   Licensor shall have the right, at its own expense (subject to the last sentence of this clause (b)), on at least thirty (30) days prior written notice to Distributor, to have a certified public accountant examine the books of account with regard to the exploitation of the Picture at Distributor's principal place of business during normal business hours, but not more than once annually and for not more than one consecutive thirty (30) day period during each annual period (provided that the books and records are timely made available to such auditor). Such right of examination shall be limited solely to inspection of books and records pertaining to the Picture (and no information related to allocations of revenues or expenses shall be redacted from such books and records) for the period three years prior to the date of the most recent statement provided by Distributor.

6.   DISTRIBUTION AND MARKETING: Distributor shall have complete discretion and control as to the time, manner and terms of distribution, exhibition, licensing, exploitation, advertising and marketing of the Picture (including the unrestricted right to use sublicensees or subdistributors, except for the initial theatrical distribution of the Picture), including without limitation any decision to make the Picture available for video-on-demand exhibition day and date with the theatrical release of the Picture; provided, however, that Distributor shall consult with Licensor with respect to the marketing strategy for the initial theatrical release of the Picture, it being understood and agreed that Distributor's decisions shall be controlling with respect to all such matters. Distributor makes no guarantees, warranties or representations as to the amount of Net Receipts that may be derived from the Picture. **[Always get a marketing plan and commitment; always drill down into when there are any sub-distributors and try to avoid middlemen as discussed above]**

7.   CREDITS:

(a)   Distributor shall have the right, at its expense, to include its (or any of its affiliates, subdistributors, or licensees) names, logos, trademarks and/or emblems, in such manner, position and form as Distributor may elect and is customary in the motion picture industry (including a presentation credit), on all prints and copies of the Picture and on all advertising and publicity materials for the Picture, together with all appropriate text, as determined by Distributor in its sole discretion, indicating that the Picture is being distributed by Distributor.

(b)   Distributor shall adhere to Licensor's contractual credit and paid advertising obligations to third parties and shall notify the licensees of Distributor with regard to such obligations, provided that Distributor receives timely written notice of such obligations and that such obligations are reasonable and customary in the motion picture industry. The casual or inadvertent failure by Distributor or the failure of any third party to comply with such obligations shall not be a breach hereof. Within a reasonable period following receipt of written notice from Licensor specifying the details of any failure by Distributor or any licensee of Distributor to comply with contractual credit or paid advertising obligations, Distributor will notify any applicable licensee regarding such failure and will take such steps as are reasonably and economically practicable to cure such failure prospectively with respect to copies of the Picture not yet made and advertisements for the Picture issued by or under the control of Distributor which have not yet been placed.

8.   COPYRIGHT: The copyright in the Picture will be held by Licensor, and Licensor shall register, renew, extend and protect such copyright in Licensor's name for the maximum period of time allowed by law and furnish Distributor with copies of such registrations. If Licensor fails to do so, Distributor shall have the right to register the copyright in Producer's name in the U.S. Copyright Office, the cost of which shall be a Distribution Expense. In addition, Distributor shall have the right, subject to prior consultation with Licensor, to take such steps and to institute such suits and proceedings as Distributor may deem necessary or advisable to protect the copyright in the Picture and its elements and to prevent any infringement of the Granted Rights, all of which costs shall be deemed Distribution Expenses, provided that any and all recoveries shall be included in the gross receipts for purposes of calculating Net Receipts. Licensor shall have the right to participate in any such legal proceedings with counsel of its choice at its expense. In connection with the foregoing, Licensor hereby irrevocably appoints Distributor as its attorney- in-fact with the full power to execute any and all documents as may reasonably required consistent with the terms of this Agreement. This appointment shall be a power coupled with an interest. Distributor shall provide copies to Licensor of any material documents executed by Distributor pursuant to such power of attorney.

[Always try to retain copyright in a distribution deal]

9.   DELIVERY: **[OMITTED because it varies too much]**

10.   EDITING AND MODIFICATIONS: Distributor shall have the right to cut, edit, delete from, dub and subtitle the Picture as Distributor in its sole discretion shall determine is necessary: (a) to subtitle or dub the Picture as is customary for exploitation of the Picture; (b) to avoid legal liability; (c) to conform the Picture to meet the requirements of a governmental censorship authority or comply with local or national broadcast standards or any other applicable laws or standards (including obscenity laws or standards); (d) to create closed caption versions; (e) to insert bugs, advertising, sponsorships or other commercial materials (including, without limitation, such promotional and commercial material that may run concurrently with the end credits); (f) to squeeze and compress the film and the credits in a manner which is then current in the motion picture and television industries; (g) to create promotional materials; and (h) to create and license clips from the Picture in a manner which is

customary in the motion picture and television industries, and/or to authorize any person to do the foregoing. With respect to any editing of the Picture for the purposes set forth in clauses (b) or (c), or in any manner other than as described in this Paragraph, such editing shall be subject to the written approval of Licensor, provided that if Licensor has failed to respond to Distributor within 5 business days after receipt of Distributor's notice of requested editing or if Licensor accepts such offer but is not ready and willing to do so when reasonably required by Distributor, such editing shall be deemed approved and Distributor shall have the right to make such edits or to cause a third party to make such edits. **[Sometimes editing is needed to get on to TV or airlines so you'll need to allow that but of course you'll want to try to get approval of any substantive editing for ratings or any other kind.]**

11.   DEFERRED FEES; RESIDUALS: The calculation and payment of any and all residuals, deferred fees and/or third party participations shall be the responsibility of Licensor alone. The Picture is not under the jurisdiction of any guild and Distributor shall have no guild residual obligations. **[Some distributors and studios will assume this responsibility]**

12.   SECURITY INTEREST: As security for the rights and entitlements of Distributor hereunder, Licensor hereby grants and assigns to Distributor a mortgage of copyright and a continuing security interest in all of Licensor's right, title and interest in and to the Granted Rights hereunder and all proceeds thereof. Licensor agrees to execute all such documents as Distributor may reasonably require in order to effectuate the security interest, including the Mortgage of Copyright and Power of Attorney attached hereto as Exhibit C. **[Intellectual Property is indeed treated like property and thus a security interest is a property interest (in this case your film Copyright is the property, mortgaged as collateral as it were). I rarely agree to this type of security interest provision in a distribution deal (an investment agreement would be different or the filmmaker having a security interest in the film where rights were granted to the distributor would also be different). Only reason to agree to it in the context of a distribution deal is if the distributor wants to be protected from you not paying union payment obligations (such as SAG) because guilds will come after distributor but then the security interest protects the distributor but should be limited and only for that purpose and in that scenario.]**

13.   LICENSOR DEFAULT: At Distributor's option and upon written notice given to Licensor, Distributor shall have the right to terminate this Agreement and shall be entitled to immediate repayment of all out-of-pocket costs incurred by Distributor in connection with the Picture and may declare all obligations hereunder due and owing and may proceed to enforce payment and performance by Licensor and exercise all of Distributor's rights and remedies at law or equity, if (i) Licensor breaches any material covenant, agreement or obligation under this Agreement and fails to cure such breach within forty-eight (48) hours after receipt of written notice from Distributor (except such right to cure shall not apply to Licensor's failure to timely deliver the Picture by

the Delivery Date in accordance with Paragraph 9(b)); (ii) any representation or warranty made by Licensor is untrue or incomplete in any material respect on or as of the date made; or (iii) Licensor becomes insolvent or a petition under any bankruptcy or insolvency law shall be filed by or against Licensor or any property of Licensor is attached and such attachment is not released within 30 days or if Licensor executes an assignment for the benefit of creditors or if a receiver, custodian, liquidator or trustee is appointed for Licensor. Without limiting any other remedies available to it hereunder or by law, Distributor shall have the right to withhold and reserve from any monies whatsoever payable to Licensor hereunder, sums reasonably sufficient to secure Distributor from and against Licensor's liabilities or the material breach of any of its obligations under this Agreement. **[Any default provision should go both ways and cover you too in case of Distributor default. You definitely want protection in case distributor materially breaches, defaults, files bankruptcy, becomes insolvent, stops distributing films.]**

14.   REPRESENTATIONS, WARRANTIES AND INDEMNITIES: Licensor hereby represents and warrants that (i) it has the full right, power and authority to enter into this Agreement and to grant the rights granted herein, (ii) Licensor owns or controls all rights in and to the Picture and in and to all literary, dramatic and musical material included therein required for Distributor to exercise the Granted Rights, without any lien, claim or other encumbrance thereon, (iii) all musical compositions and/or performances of musical compositions contained in the Picture have been licensed for in- context use, out-of-context use (including use in advertising and publicity of the Picture and the DVD menu)) in all media, now known, worldwide, for the duration of the License Period, and no additional payment for the use of any such composition or performance shall be required except for payment of the applicable performance rights fees to ASCAP, BMI or SESAC, if applicable, and payment of new use or re- use fees in connection with master recordings, if applicable, (iv) all licenses of any material licensed for use in connection with the Picture contain language to the substantive effect that the licensor of such material has not and shall not commit any act likely to prevent or hinder the full enjoyment of the rights that are licensed hereunder, (v) no part of the Picture nor the exhibition, distribution, exploitation, promotion or other use of the Picture by Distributor or its licensees will violate or infringe upon any rights of any third party, (vi) there are no guilds or unions that may claim jurisdiction over the services to be rendered hereunder and no collective bargaining agreements covering the Picture, and (vii) there is no action, suit, claim or proceeding pending, affecting or threatened against the Picture, its producers, Licensor or any distributor of the Picture. Licensor shall indemnify, defend (at Distributor's election), and hold harmless Distributor and its officers, agents, employees, affiliates, licensees and assigns from and against any and all claims, damages, liabilities, costs and expenses, including reasonable outside attorneys' fees and disbursements, arising out of (A) any breach or, in connection with a third party claim, alleged breach of any representation, warranty, covenant or agreement made by Licensor herein, (B) the exercise by Distributor of the Granted Rights in accordance with this Agreement, or (C) the violation or infringement of the rights of any third party as a result of the

exhibition, distribution, exploitation, promotion or other use of the Picture by Distributor or its licensees in accordance with this Agreement. **[Standard for such provisions to be in many film and television agreements. Make sure you read carefully and can truly warrant and represent what is noted. Sometimes you may want the warranty and representation by you to be qualified as to be "to the best of [your] knowledge. Any indemnification language should be mutual.]**

15.   INSURANCE: Licensor shall (at its own cost and expense) provide and maintain, in full force and effect for a period of three years from Delivery, a liability insurance (errors and omissions coverage) policy or policies that covers any and all claims arising out of or relating to errors and omissions related to media liability for the Picture and the title thereof with a deductible of no more than $10,000 and with minimum limits of at least $1,000,000 for any claim arising out of single occurrence and $3,000,000 in the aggregate for the Picture. Licensor shall name Distributor, its parent, affiliates, subsidiaries, assigns and licensees as now or hereafter may exist as additional insureds on such policy.

[Very common provision and platforms such as Netflix requires this too. If you have not gotten E&O insurance see if the distributor will get it and then recoup the actual cost; or maybe the distributor will be willing to just rely on the company umbrella policy.]

16.   MISCELLANEOUS:

(a)   Distributor shall have the right to assign its rights and obligations hereunder to any third party and shall be relieved of its obligations to the extent they are assumed in writing by (i) any purchaser of all or substantially all of its stock or assets, (ii) any entity into which it is merged, consolidated or combined, (iii) any mini or major studio, or (iv) any affiliate of Distributor. Distributor shall have the right to assign its rights and obligations hereunder to any other third party not listed in clauses (i) through (iv) above, provided that Distributor shall remain primarily liable to Licensor for its obligations hereunder unless prior written approval of such assignment and assumption of Distributor's rights and obligations is obtained from Licensor. Licensor may not assign this Agreement or any of its rights or obligations hereunder, other than its right to receive monies hereunder, without the prior written approval of Distributor (not to be unreasonably withheld). [I try to limit assignment to only either a company approved by client in writing or if there is a merger of the distributor with another company (as contemplated in the language above). Try to have the original distributor always remain liable for any obligations (also covered in the above language). Some contracts have language that does not require the company to remain secondarily liable where the assignment is to a major studio.]

(b)   THIS AGREEMENT SHALL BE GOVERNED BY AND CONSTRUED IN ACCORDANCE WITH THE LAWS OF THE STATE OF XYZ APPLICABLE TO CONTRACTS MADE AND WHOLLY PERFORMED

THEREIN WITHOUT REGARD TO PRINCIPLES OF CONFLICTS OF LAW. EACH PARTY HEREBY CONSENTS TO THE JURISDICTION OF ANY STATE OR FEDERAL COURT LOCATED IN THE STATE OF ILLINOIS, CITY OF CHICAGO. **[All agreements will have what is called a "Choice of Law" and "Venue" provision that determines what law governs the contract (either a non-US country (e.g. Canada, United Kingdom, Italy, Israel) or a U.S. state (e.g. New York, California, Delaware) usually. This matters because laws vary and so you will want to be informed about that impact on you should there be a dispute. If it's between you and a company you won't have leverage enough to have this provision changes most likely except for maybe venue where you can agree to a venue mutually convenient, in between you, but it' srare for companies to change the provision that describes the law that will govern the agreement and/or the venue for any disputes. Very often companies have an arbitration clause that requires private arbitration of any disputes instead of litigation in court. Sometimes informal mediation will be a required first step that at least gives the parties a chance to try to resolve things for free and with less hassle. There are various arbitration forums and companies often pick ones that are pro-companies but this is a legitimate forum for dispute resolution and although it is not free, it is cheaper than litigation and again, private. The privacy aspect may work to your disadvantage if negative publicity from a lawsuit would have been good negotiating leverage. Also look out for an attorneys' fees provision whereby the prevailing party gets their attorneys' fees and costs covered by the opposing and losing party. This can work for or hurt you – depending on whether you prevail.)**

(c)   Licensor agrees that its rights and remedies in the event of any breach of this Agreement by Distributor will be limited to the right, if any, to recover money damages in an action at law, and in no event will Licensor be entitled by reason of any such breach to seek injunctive or other equitable relief or to enjoin or restrain the distribution, exhibition. advertising or any other means of exploitation of the Picture or the Granted Rights, except to the extent the Distributor exceeds the scope of the Granted Rights. **[It is extremely common for companies to have you limit your relief to damages at law (money) and waive any right to injunctive relief (having the company do or not do something, e.g. start or stop production or, as applicable to this example, stop or start distribution). Pay attention to this provision and at certain times you may want to fight this where you have leverage and where some injunctive relief would truly be warranted (e.g. fixing credits).]**

(d)   This Agreement may not be amended nor any provision waived except in writing signed by the pees hereto. This Agreement contains the full understanding of the parties with respect to the subject matter hereof and supersedes any and all previous agreements between the parties. Each party acknowledges that it is entering into this Agreement in reliance only upon the provisions herein set forth, and not upon any representation, warranty, covenant, agreement, obligation or other consideration nor set forth herein. [This is critical. It's called an Integration Clause or a Merger Clause and is meant to exclude what is called Parol Evidence (evidence outside the contract, especially that about any dealings and agreements or discussions before the contact was entered into. This matters because all contracts written by an attorney will have this provision and that means to avoid conflict and drama, you had better make sure all the promises made to you that enticed you to get into the contract are IN THE CONTRACT. Don't sign a contract without all that you are relying on, hoping, expecting, etc., being written down in the final agreement. Trust me when I tell you that otherwise, problems are likely to ensue. Remember that Choice of Law provision above? Well California and New York have different rules about Parol Evidence so remember that these provisions are not just random gobbildy gook. They can have real serious consequences when you least expect it.

(e) All notices from either party to the other in connection herewith shall be given in writing by international courier, messenger, facsimile or personal delivery, addressed to the parties as first set forth above. The earlier of (i) actual receipt (ii) five days after the date of the receipt from an International courier, and (iii) the date of messengering, faxing (providing there is an electronic "answerback") or of personal delivery shall be deemed to be the date of service. **[I think we can all agree that faxing is dead. If you see a reference to Notices via carrier pigeon, RUN! In all seriousness, consider adding Notice via email and that email constitutes a "writing" but that can go both ways which means that if this was agreed to, you would have to be sure to read your email frequently enough to notice any Notice.]**

(f) This Agreement is comprised of this document as well as Exhibits A, B and C and Schedules 1 and 2, all of which Exhibits and Schedules are incorporated by this reference. **[Including Delivery Exhibits and the like is beyond the scope of this book and thus we have excluded them.]**

By signing in the places below, Distributor and Licensor accept and agree to all the terms and conditions of this Agreement as of the date of execution.

YYY PRODUCTIONS   **XXX DISTRIBUTION**

By: By:

_____   _____
Name   Name
Title   Title

_____   _____
Date Signed   Date Signed

Roberta Marie Munroe

PRODUCER | AUTHOR | DIRECTOR | CONSULTANT

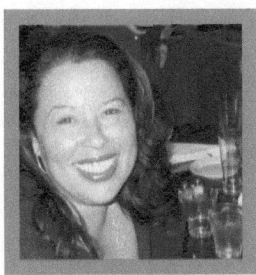

Ms. Munroe is currently writing, directing, and producing a documentary series, *Charleston 2016,* a project partially funded by the state of South Carolina, as well the pilot, *The Day My Boobs Left,* with writer/director Michele Martinelli. Roberta has produced over 30 short films, and 3 features including:

- *Warrior Road* – feature narrative starring brothers Lorenzo & David Henrie (The Walking Dead), writer/director Brad Jayne, executive produced by Denis Gallagher & Charliewood Pictures.

- *ToY* - feature narrative starring Briana Evigan and Kerry Norton, writer/director Pat Chapman, Cinequest FF, FilmOut (winner of Best Performance).

- *The Parker Tribe* – TV pilot/short film starring *SNL's* Paula Pell, Tribeca 2015, Palm Springs ShortsFest, Outfest, Best Comedy Short LA Shortsfest 2015, and best comedy pilot at the 2015 New York Television Festival.

- *Irene & Marie* – Starring Olympia Dukakis and Rose Gregario. Newport FF 2015; writer/director Alex Thompson.

- *The Procession* – Starring Lily Tomlin & Jesse Tyler Ferguson - Palm Springs 2012, Tribeca 2012, "Stars In Shorts" Theatrical release 2013 writer/director Rob Festinger.

- *Debutante Hunters* – Audience Award, Sundance 2012, Palm Springs ShortsFest 2011, writer/director Maria White.

- *Suicide Canaries* – SXSW 2010, writers/directors Natalia Provatas and Valerian Zamel.

OTHER TITLES INCLUDE: *Sketch* (Audience Award, Urbanworld 2014, Jury Prize, PanAfrican FF 2015, Audience Award Breckenridge 2015); *Letter to God* (World Premiere and Audience Award, DC Shorts 2015); *Only Fair* (DC Shorts Fest 2013); *Plus Ultra* (DC Shorts Fest 2013); *My Night With Andrew Cunanan* (Frameline 2012, Melbourne LGBT Film Festival 2012,

Cleveland International FF 2012, Iris Prize Nominee 2012)

Ms. Munroe is the author of *How Not To Make A Short Film: Secrets From A Sundance Programmer*, (Hyperion 2009). The 2nd Edition Audiobook, read by the author, was published by Hachette Books - January 2015. The book has been translated to Chinese (2015 Big Apple Publishing, Beijing) and Korean (Communications Books, Seoul 2013), and its translation and publication in Spanish is in negotiation. Roberta is currently finishing on her second book, *How Not To Sign A Film Contract*, that will provide filmmakers with an overview of film industry contractual law with a publish date of September 2016.

As a director, Roberta recently completed *The Sibling Code* (Oxford FF, Blackstar FF, Nantucket FF, Sidewalk FF 2016) and wrote and directed the award-winning short film *Dani & Alice*, a 35mm film project of the Fox Searchlight Director's Lab, that went on to win several Best Short awards worldwide. Her comedy *Happy Birthday* also won several Best Short Awards and both films were distributed by Wolfe Releasing via DVD and Netflix. She wrote, directed and produced two shorts commissioned by the UNFPA (United Nations), *Maja* and *Family Prayers* with a specific focus on children, women, and reproductive rights in Egypt and Eastern Europe.

As a film festival consultant & programmer, Roberta has programmed film at IFP New York (No Borders co-production market section), Tampa LGBT FF, and spent 5 years programming at the Sundance Film Festival. She was the Sales & Industry Theatre Manager at the Toronto International Film Festival (TIFF), and Managing Director of the Niagara International Film Festival (NIFF – Niagara on the Lake).

Roberta is highly respected and beloved by filmmakers all over the world as a true champion of artists.

You can often find Roberta hanging in Palm Springs or Los Angeles, California, sipping an ice-cold martini, with her two rescue dogs Marcello & Rita.

CONTACT: robertamunroe@gmail.com

Orly Ravid
ENTERTAINMENT ATTORNEY I FOUNDER/CO-EXECUTIVE
DIRECTOR OF THE FILM COLLABORATIVE

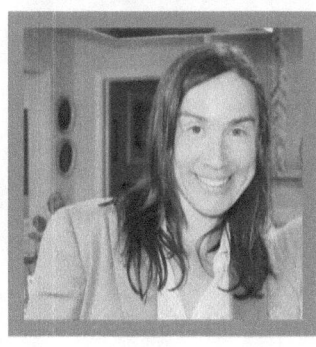

Orly Ravid, born in Israel and raised in Manhattan, is an entertainment attorney in Los Angeles at MSK (Mitchell Silberberg & Knupp LLP) and is the founder/co-executive director of the distribution non-profit The Film Collaborative (TFC). Non-profit on purpose, TFC specializes in distribution of documentaries and arthouse cinema without taking filmmakers' rights. TFC also co-authored and published the case study book series *Selling Your Film Without Selling Your Soul*.

Orly has a 16-year career in independent film as an executive and consultant in business affairs, all aspects of distribution, domestic and international sales/licensing, development, production, and grassroots marketing. Orly regularly speaks at film school and film festival panels about film distribution, new media, splitting rights and legal concerns facing filmmakers.

A lover of film, filmmakers, and artists, Orly first started trying to write screenplays and working at film festivals. She was also a Programming Associate for documentaries at Sundance and advised its Artist Services initiative. Orly was also a programming consultant for Palm Springs International and the Middle East International Film Festival.

Orly graduated from Columbia University with her Bachelor's degree in English Literature, with a film concentration. Her legal background includes a full-tuition scholarship to Southwestern Law School (housing one of the best entertainment law programs in the country), judicial clerkships and an externship at the California Supreme Court. Orly wrote two entertainment-related amicus appellate law briefs, one to the United States Supreme Court which held in accordance with the position Orly advocated.

Presently, Orly's legal practice is centered around entertainment law and representing filmmakers, mostly in transactions but sometimes litigation as well. The transactions Orly works on include option purchase agreements for books and screenplays, distribution and licensing deals, co-production deals, film financing, and rights clearances, to name a few.

Orly is committed to providing filmmakers with sustainable and equitable distribution and bringing to her practice of law TFC's philosophies and transparent methodologies. Orly is committed to her wife and cats, named Kitten and Mr. Cat.

CONTACT: For more information about TFC, its mission and distribution services and Orly's legal practice go to: thefilmcollaborative.org & msk.com. You also can find Orly on some social media.

"I am a pretty versatile fool when it comes to contracts, and business and such things. I have signed a lot of contracts in my time, and at sometime I probably knew what the contracts meant, but six months later everything had grown dim and I could be *certain* of only two things, to wit:

One, I didn't sign any contract.
Two, the contract means the opposite of what it says."
- Mark Twain's Notebook

Michelle Mower
WRITER I PRODUCER I DIRECTOR I IMAGINATION WORLDWIDE

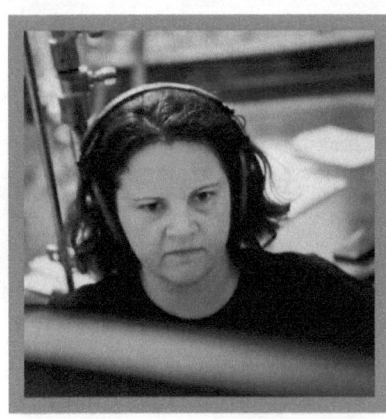 Michelle Mower is an internationally- acclaimed motion picture writer, producer, and director whose debut feature film *The Preacher's Daughter*, starring Andrea Bowen (*Desperate Housewives*) premiered on Lifetime Movie Network (LMN) in 2012.

The premiere garnered the highest ratings of any movie on LMN for the year and launched a franchise of "preacher"-themed films for the network, as well as a reality series. Michelle has since written and directed two more made-for-TV movies for A&E/Lifetime. In addition, Michelle produced the independent feature film *Dreamer* that was subsequently licensed to NUVO television.

Michelle recently acquired Imagination Worldwide, an international film sales and distribution company based in Los Angeles. The company is currently developing a slate of story-driven movies targeted to female audiences.

Michelle received her Bachelor's degree in Radio/Television from the University in Houston in 2000. After graduation,

Michelle was hired by the Houston NBC affiliate as Associate Producer for the morning news program. In 2003, Michelle went to work for Southwest Alternate Media Project (SWAMP), a nonprofit media arts organization based in Houston. Her primary function as Program Coordinator was to organize. SWAMP's professional development workshops, youth after-school programs, independent film screenings, monthly networking mixers and special film-related events. Through her work with SWAMP, Michelle started *Lights! Camera! Action!* Summer Moviemaking Camp for teens and the annual Business of Film Conference, which takes place annually at Rice University.

Michelle is heavily involved in the film community in Texas. She previously served on the boards of Texas Motion Picture Alliance (TXMPA) and Women In Film and Television (WiFT). She currently sits on the board for Southwest Alternate Media Project (SWAMP), 4th Wall Theatre Company, and the advisory board for Houston Community College's Department of Film and Audio Production.

Kathy Susca
EDITOR I MEMBERSHIP COORDINATOR FOR TFC

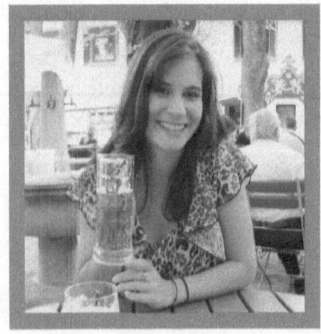

Kathy Susca is honored to serve as the editor of *How Not to Sign a Film Contract*. In 2011, she graduated from USC with a dual major in film criticism and Italian. She went on to NYU for her Master's in Cinema Studies, and came back to sunny LA after graduation. She has been the Membership Coordinator at The Film Collaborative since 2013. Kathy lives with her Italian boyfriend and their beloved basil plant, Francesco. You can reach her at kathy@thefilmcollaborative.org.